Horses in Shakespeare's England

Horses in Shakespeare's England

Anthony Dent

J. A. Allen
London

First published in Great Britain by
J. A. Allen & Co Ltd
1 Lower Grosvenor Place
Buckingham Palace Road
London SW1W 0EL
1987

British Library Cataloguing in Publication Data

Dent, Anthony
Horses in Shakespeare's England.
1. Horses – England – History
I. Title
636.1'00942   SF284.G7

ISBN 0 85131 441 4

Printed in Great Britain by the Bath Press, Avon

Contents

Acknowledgements

My thanks are due to the Marquess of Salisbury for granting me the facilities to study the Cecil Papers, and to my kinsman Robin Harcourt Williams, archivist and librarian at Hatfield House, for guiding my hand in that luckiest of lucky dips.

The author and publishers would also like to thank the following for permission to reproduce the photographs: Board of Trustees of the Victoria and Albert Museum; Bodleian Library, Oxford; The British Library; College of Arms; Courtauld Institute of Art; Crawford Films; Edinburgh University Library; Harrap Limited, London; Koninklijk Museum voor Schone Kunsten, Antwerp; Kunstmuseum, Basel; the Marquess of Salisbury; Miland Publishers, Nieuwkoop, Netherlands; Musées Royaux de Beaux-Arts, Brussels; National Museum of Wales, Cardiff; Prado Museum, Madrid; St Faith's Church, Gaywood, King's Lynn; Syndics of Cambridge University Library; and the Trustees of the British Museum.

Quotations from Shakespeare's works and line numbers follow the Arden edition.

Preface

I do not subscribe to the view that the Dark Lady of Shakespeare's Sonnets was a black or even a brown mare, any more than that she was the Earl of Southampton, or Lucy Negro of Wapping, or Christopher Marlowe's bedmaker at Corpus. And if the Sonnets are really to be counted as the most subjective and personal of Shakespeare's writings, then the conceit about riding towards and away from his love in Sonnets L and LI tells us very little about the poet's personality or that of his horse. Indeed, at the period in question he may very well have had no horse, since of all the hundreds of references to horses and horsemen that he made, this is among the most generalised and least concrete.

One cannot pretend that a single one of these references tells us anything about the writer's attitude to horses or to a particular kind of horse, or claim that it affords the slightest clue to his nature. What they do afford, collectively, is a view of an important aspect of life in his country and his time, an indispensable part of its material civilisation. Nowadays knowledge about such things is confined to a minority, a 'special interest group', who are in general so little regarded by the learned that their advice is never asked in cases where it might be helpful. The learned glossator will cheerfully write 'fives, a disease of horses' without explaining *which* disease; or gloss 'riggish' as wanton without thinking it worthwhile to explain that it qualifies, literally, the behaviour of a rig – he has moved so much further away from the horse-borne world than his counterpart of Shakespeare's day as not even to know what a rig is.

In this book, the first part of each chapter or section (introduced by the horse motif) explains the separate elements of the all-pervading equestrian culture of Shakespeare's England that has been driven into a small corner of modern Western society. The second part of the chapter or section (introduced by the book motif) shows how such commonplaces of Shakespeare's life, that are no longer commonplaces of ours, are illustrated in his works. Together, it is hoped, these parts will form a tool for the literal interpretation of passages whose physical meaning becomes less and less clear to each successive generation of playgoers. From this they are at liberty to deduce less literal meanings. But to do the latter need not be the labour of your obedient servant.

St Pierre-de-Chignac
Dordogne

                                                            ANTHONY DENT

Danby Dale
North Yorkshire

LAURENCE OLIVIER.

12th October 1987

A horse! A horse! My Kingdom for a horse!
                              RICHARD III

Today we have so many diverse methods of transport
that it is difficult to visualise an age which
depended entirely on the horse for mobility.

Anthony Dent's masterly exposition of the role of
the horse in Shakespeare's day, and its influence
on the life and work of the Bard, will delight and
educate horselovers and historians alike, whilst,
at the same time, adding greatly to the understanding
of Shakespeare's plays and Shakespearian language in
general.

Nor should the casual reader be deterred from reading
this book, for it is that rare thing - a work of
scholarship that is as entertaining as it is erudite.

Oliviery

LORD OLIVIER

1

The language of horsemanship

It has become almost obligatory for the contributor of any item of Shakespeariana to declare at the outset who he thinks Shakespeare was. I therefore solemnly affirm that I believe the author of the corpus of plays and poems commonly known as the Works of William Shakespeare to have been none other than the boy from Stratford of that name, of whose life much is known. What is more, the sum total of all the references to horses and horsemanship in the said works tends to support the view that they were written by the well-authenticated William Shakespeare of Stratford, or if not by him then by someone of exactly the same social background or class who had had exactly the same education and upbringing. For all or most of the persons reputed by some to be the real authors of the Works were of a social class and educational background that would have produced a somewhat different picture of the equestrian world from the one we have in the plays. Certainly a Baconian view would have differed greatly.

Commentators, and especially non-academic commentators, on this aspect of the plays comprise two extreme factions. Those who know nothing about horses are impressed by the enormous amount that Shakespeare did know, and are inclined to seek explanation for this by some unrecorded aspect of his life that would have given him such special knowledge. The others, who know a great deal about horses and horsemanship as they are in our time, are apt to point out how little he knew, and how wrong he was about this point and that, often implying their belief that he may well have been equally wrong on a great many other matters about which their own knowledge does not extend far enough to arm their criticism.

The fact is that knowledge of these subjects apparent in the works is exactly of the amount and kind that we should expect to find in the mental equipment of a middle-class provincial whose youth had been spent in close contact with the countryside, who had worked in London, and who had not attended a university but had such acquaintance with classical authors as might be attained by rubbing shoulders with university people and by reading such translations of the classics as were being more and more abundantly printed for London booksellers at the time.

A certain minimum of information on horses was inescapable, in Shakespeare's England, for all classes of the population. The proportion of Englishmen who could not ride at all was about the same as the proportion of Englishmen today who cannot ride a bicycle: certainly smaller than the proportion who cannot drive a car. Of what must be done to keep a horse in working order, only two strata of the population were ignorant: the very rich and powerful, and those of the poor whose work had never brought them into close contact with horses – and there were very few menial jobs for men that did not do this, at one time or another. After all, the contemporary definition of a down-and-out was a man who holds horses for other people. Indeed, one of Shakespeare's detractors jeered at him in print for having held playgoers' horses outside the theatre itself. The casual horse-holder occupied that position in society now filled by the self-appointed car-park attendant and casual car-washer. He was the grateful recipient of six-penny tips if his client were a lord, as we see in the household accounts of the Cecils at Hatfield, in which *curat de minimis* is a maxim rather than something not done. 'To a man, sixpence, for walking my lord's horse' occurs there many times. No doubt clients of lesser degree would bestow copper down to a halfpenny (but in those days one could buy a drink, of a sort, for a halfpenny). Horse-holding, and more still horse-walking, with strange animals, does require a certain minimum of skill and practice.

The children of the rich and powerful were taught to ride as a matter of course, and when they were grown up they never walked anywhere. But they were not necessarily taught anything at all about horsemastership, and its practice entered not at all into their ideology. Mucking out was for menials, and amongst the ethics knocked into the pate of the Elizabethan young master by way of his buttocks there was no pious Pony Club nonsense about the moral implications of diligent wielding of the dung fork and the wheelbarrow. Riding was all the contact such people had with horses. Petruchio in *The Taming of the Shrew* expresses it most clearly:

> What, no man at door
> To hold my stirrup nor to take my horse?   (IV, i, 107)

The horse was brought to my lord's door; he rode for whatever purpose was in hand that day; he came home, dismounted, and the horse was led away, not to be seen by him again until the next time he needed it.

But it is characteristic of the English economy of the sixteenth and seventeenth centuries that ownership of horses should stretch a long way down the social scale. This is partly due to the fact that despite the much-publicised enclosures there was still a great deal of common land attached to most townships, so that grazing of a sort was not difficult to come by. In the inventories taken by the executors of small husbandmen, tenants rather than freeholders, and tradesmen of equivalent economic status, one frequently finds that the value of horses owned comes to something like 10 per cent of the total chattel estate, and saddlery about 5 per cent; very often the entire wearing apparel of the deceased is worth less than his saddle and bridle. I once saw, in such a will from Yorkshire, a bequest of 'the half part of a nag, and a two-year-old filly'. Reference to the inventory attached showed that this half-share in a riding-horse and a filly was valued at £4 3s 4d. But the whole estate, in moveable goods, was worth little more than £20.

It is also true that by contrast with our age there were servants in households of very modest means, both in town and country, and the employment in particular of manservants had not yet come to imply superior social status. But obviously the best servants gravitated to the superior establishments, and 'lived with' masters who lived better, quite apart from the question of wages. Poorer employers got more than their share of idle, stupid, clumsy, sickly and above all drunken servants. Add to this the fact that there were few middle-class occupations that could be effectively carried on without the use of at least one horse, and we arrive at a combination of circumstances in which the sons of middle-class families in a town like Stratford would come in for a great deal of stable-work. John Shakespeare as an agricultural merchant had to be constantly on horseback, buying off the farms, and no doubt at the height of his prosperity had stablemen who were equal to their duties. But as his fortunes began to decline, he would probably only be able to afford the sort who are never fit for work on Monday morning, and eventually none at all. In such circumstances the care of Bayard falls inevitably on the sons of the house; and when William left home to take up his apprenticeship this sort of duty would still fall to him, since in all trades the care of the master's horse was among the duties of his apprentices. 'Knowing about horses' was regarded in the mid twentieth century as something characteristic of the rural gentry; but in the late sixteenth century it was equally characteristic of the urban bourgeoisie. A man could not 'get on', in any sense of the phrase, without the use of horses, and yet until he 'got on' a good way he and his family must take a hand in the work which the use of horses entails.

This store of practical knowledge was supplemented, in the mind of a born self-educator, by a great deal of theoretical 'knowledge' derived second-hand from such classic authors as Pliny or Varro. The great certainties of the ancient world about the physical nature of the universe, about natural history and its orderly conformance with the scheme of the four elements had not been challenged in Shakespeare's time. Now it has been knocked endways and replaced by a new, if constantly changing, body of scientific knowledge in those fields which affect veterinary practice from anatomy to the pharmacopoeia. Similarly, because of lack of apparatus necessary for clinical observation, what passed for observed phenomena then will not serve our generation of physical experimenters. Because nobody in the England of that day – not even a knacker – had ever totally dissected a horse, Shakespeare and his contemporaries had no reason to doubt the following diagnosis and cure of a disease called by his fellow-writer Gervase Markham

> The Cords . . . that maketh a horse stumble and many times fall, and they appear in the horse's forelegs, this is the cure thereof. Take a sharp knife and cut a slitte even at the tip his nose, just with the point of the grisle, open the slit being made and you shall perceive a white string, take it up with a boar's tooth or some crooked bodkin, and cut it asunder, then stich up the slitte and anoint it with butter and the horse doubtless shall be recovered.

Doubtless. What was truth to them is not necessarily truth to us now, and it is the traces of such beliefs found in the works of Shakespeare that make the modern reader, knowledgeable about horses, write him off as one abysmally ignorant of the subject.

In so far as the author's knowledge of horses and of animal-powered transport is embodied in the action and dialogue of his works as reality, as something actually narrated or described, it needs no comment here. But the manner in which, and the reasons why, this matter is so frequently used in forming figures of speech, some traditional and some original, call for an explanation.

Image, metaphor and proverb
Even if the works of Shakespeare contained no literal, physical mention of horses and the work of various kinds done by them, they would still be plentifully sprinkled throughout with purely ornamental animals, serving to embellish his language. Among these, a few no doubt are of the author's own breeding; but they were already so plentiful that he could get what he wanted any week on market day, at Stratford or Smithfield or anywhere else that the English language was current.

To take that language as he found it: a common stock of proverbial expressions then current was listed by a contemporary, William Camden, a Londoner by birth but by parentage a Midlander like Shakespeare and Samuel Johnson, his father having been born at Lichfield in Staffordshire. His mother came from the Curwens of Workington in Cumbria, a family which generations later owned the celebrated

Curwen Barb, one of the respected founding fathers of the General Stud Book. Proverbs and such ornaments of speech are something we commonly inherit from our parents nowadays, but until recently, and certainly in the sixteenth century, were something passed on to children by their grandparents, with whom, especially at the Camden/Shakespeare level of middle-class society, children passed much more of their time than they do now. Thus the thesaurus of such sayings printed in Camden's *Remains* probably represents what was current when his grandparents were young, in the last years of Henry VII's reign (Camden having been born in 1551), at which time also Shakespeare's grandparents were young. Many sayings can be proved to be of much older coinage, for they are quoted in almost the same words as in those fascinating dialogues between people 'riding by the way' with which Chaucer interspersed his pilgrims' tales. Here is a brief selection of Camden's figures of speech relating to horses:

1. A grunting horse and a groaning wife never fail their master.
2. A proud horse that will not bear his own provender.
3. A scald horse is good enough for a scabbed squire.
4. A short horse is soon curried.
5. He that is mann'd with boys and hors'd with colts shall have his meat eaten and his work undone.
6. How can the fole amble when the horse and mare trot?
7. It's ill to set spurs to a flying horse.
8. It's a good horse that never stumbleth.
9. Keep Bayard in the stable.
10. Look not a given horse in the mouth.
11. Many stumble at a straw, and leap over a block.
12. Of a ragged colt cometh a good horse.
13. Set a beggar on horseback, and he will gallop.
14. The eye of the master makes the horse fat.
15. The grey mare is the better horse.
16. When the steed is stolen shut the stable door.
17. Where saddles lack, better ride on a pad than on the horse bareback.
18. While the grass groweth the horse starveth.
19. Who so bold as blind Bayard?

Some of Camden's flowers of speech are a great loss to the language, inasmuch as one hears them no more: such as 'Everything helps, quoth the wren, when she piss'd in the sea.' And of those listed above, only a few are in use today, because for more than fifty years only a minority of English people have understood their literal meaning. Thus (5) is likely to have been part of the Cumbrian heritage, since in the North Country 'meat' can still mean horse feed. The meaning is the same as the couplet quoted in Chapter 3 below from *Venus and Adonis* (419) – it is a false economy to break horses to work too young, since it hampers their development and shortens their lives – and in addition they will not perform as well as a mature animal but will eat quite as much. The significance of the one about the trotting foal (6) will become clear in later chapters. The saying goes back, in written examples, to the fifteenth century, and is no more heard after the end of the seventeenth, simply because from that time onwards fewer and fewer ambling foals were either bred or sold. One wonders how many people today who make quite frequent use of saying (10) realise that one looks in the mouth to tell the age by the teeth. Stumbling at a straw (11) is quite unlikely to have applied in its literal sense to people, but its significance in terms of horses would be much greater.

Shakespeare uses this sort of 'sentence' freely, often in an elaborated form, but he also uses smaller coins of the same currency, a single word, or two or three words, whose literal significance was obvious to him, part of his everyday background. Today they are used, as often as not, by speakers who have no conception of the 'face value' or literal meaning. How many journalists who write of 'riding rough-shod' have the least idea of the nature or purpose of rough-shoeing? What is the literal meaning of 'thorough-paced'? How widely is it known that knock-down price meant a knacker's price for a horse; that easy-going meant a laterally pacing horse with a smooth action; that ear-marking was a means of identification for horses depastured on common grazings; that a shake-down, now meaning improvised sleeping quarters, is named for the action of the groom in spreading litter in a stall, itself one of the minor arts of horsemastership; that when we say Professor Purzelbaum's theory of this or that is now somewhat blown on, the literal image is of hay that has been so long in the rack that horses having nuzzled it too often do not care for it any more? A man of our time using the English language will say 'Wild horses will not drag it from me' without thinking what this really implies. Of course they could not. How are you going to harness *wild* horses to a secret or anything else? How much more realistically this verbal image was applied by Shakespeare and his contemporaries will be seen in Chapter 6 below.*

---

* There are two passages, one in a comedy and one in a tragedy, that make use of a conversational coin that has so utterly passed out of circulation as to baffle any actor of our day who tries to speak the line with conviction:
   Armado: But O, but O, —
   Moth: The hobby-horse is forgot.
   Armado: Call'st thou my love hobby-horse?
   Moth: No, master; the hobby-horse is but a colt, – and your love perhaps a hackney. But have you forgot your love? (*Love's Labour's Lost* III, i, 27)

Then there's hope a great man's memory may outlive his life half a year. But by'r lady a must build churches then, or else shall a suffer not thinking on, with the hobby-horse, whose epitaph is, 'For O, for O, the hobby-horse is forgot'. (*Hamlet* III, ii, 129)

It is plain that both Moth, page to the fantastical Spaniard Armado, and the Prince of Denmark himself are calling forth some well-known catch-phrase that must have run 'And O!, and O!, the hobby-horse is forgot'. It is very like many of the items in Camden's list of proverbial phrases but of a slightly newer minting. At this period hobby-horse can have two meanings. It can be the toy or stage-property as used in the mummers' plays,

Warwickshire is a landlocked county, and Shakespeare did not come to London, the greatest port in the kingdom and one of the greatest in Europe, till he was a grown man. But even had he been born in a seaboard shire his choice of such verbal images would not have been materially different. English figurative speech today abounds in images drawn from seafaring, dating mostly from the days of sail, though a few, such as 'full steam ahead', are of nineteenth-century coinage. It is not only in families with a naval tradition that the noisy young are requested by harassed parents to pipe down. Some of us are quite often three sheets in the wind, if not half seas over. We set sail, get under way and the wind is taken out of our sails. We are brought up all standing. A business is sunk with all hands and the cook, perhaps due to sailing too close to the wind. English people speaking or writing such phrases still have a rough idea of their literal implication, which has been recently refreshed, overall, by the increasing number of families, even those dwelling inland, who are able to indulge their pleasure in small sailing craft.

All these images are creations of the eighteenth century, or at the earliest of the late seventeenth, and it takes time for such speech habits to percolate through the entire language. Although in the days of Shakespeare England was plainly destined to become one of the greatest seafaring nations in the world, if not the greatest, the English language had not yet become so soaked in seawater and pickled in brine as it was, for example, by the time that Sheridan was writing his comedies or Smollett his novels. In Shakespeare's days, equestrian metaphors were used correctly not only by abnormally horsy people. But salty phrases were not heard, in general, except on the lips of seafaring people. For every scrap of dialogue like this of Mistress Page's:

> He would never have boarded me in this fury.
> *Mrs Ford*: 'Boarding' call you it? I'll be sure to keep him above deck.
> *Mrs Page*: So will I: if he come under my hatches, I'll never to sea again.
> (*The Merry Wives of Windsor* II, i, 85)

you will find scores of metaphorical passages, some long sustained, drawing on movement by land with the use of horses, simply because this literal use bulked so large in the experience of every English man, woman and child.

---

but it can also be a real, live animal, the hobby or hobyn of Ireland and Scotland that was later to be called a pony. And if we are to take Moth literally it is this second meaning that we must assume. It sounds as if it might be the punch-line from some once-popular anecdote about a farmer moving from one holding to another, and thinking on completion of the move that one item of his stock is missing – but not missing, for he has been sitting on it while counting the rest!

2

Mobility and power by land: the mainspring of Shakespeare's England

Drama, but especially that kind of heroic historical drama which appears to have been Shakespeare's best-selling product, requires frequent movement. Elizabethan playwrights were not confined by any such convention as the Greek unities of time and place, which by their discipline imposed a certain physically static quality, for instance, on the plots of tragedy in the classical era of the French 'court' theatre. There is not one of Shakespeare's tragedies or histories, and there are few of his comedies, that does not include a journey of considerable length on the part of some major character, and that more often by land than by sea.

The leading characters of the drama, if they are not actually reigning monarchs, are generally members of a ruling class, men of action by mere virtue of their social status, necessarily involved, all the time that the dramatist is revealing the personal pathos of their situation, in activities that we should call political. Since Shakespeare imagined the setting of all the stories that he used, no matter what country or period he derived them from, as being identical with that of the England in which he was born and grew up and accomplished his life's work, it is relevant to enquire how, in the quarter-century that covers the entire output of his writings, English monarchs, their ministers and agents and the real-life counterparts of the 'great men' who in general are the heroes of his plays moved about by land. They might be on business of state, on private journeys, or out for pleasure, including that chiefest of pleasures outdoors, then unchallenged as a recreation for a wide sector of the English social spectrum – hunting.

The Shakespearian hero, when contemplating immediate and vigorous action, is apt to call for his boots, and indeed without a recognisable pair of riding boots even the poorest theatrical wardrobe would have been gravely embarrassed, not being able to make anyone enter 'as from a journey'. But the booted and spurred character stumps off-stage as the result of an effect which has been produced by the entrance of an equally booted and spurred character, the ubiquitous and mostly anonymous Messenger. Probably few modern audiences realise that Messenger was a trade, which is why there are still families who have the word as their surname today. The immediate means whereby rulers gathered intelligence was the same as that by which they acted on it – a horse. In the appropriate chapter we shall examine the nature of the Messenger's calling, and especially those most regular messengers of all, the Posts.

Almost the one aspect of English land travel that had improved out of recognition in Shakespeare's lifetime was the postal system, and this was due to the forceful style of Tudor monarchy. The ruler must at all times be well informed and have the means by which the business of his ministers could be expeditiously done. (For 'he' read 'she' also, or even more so.) As an example of the importance of this, in the days of Queen Elizabeth's father the career of Cardinal Wolsey had taken its most decisive upward turn when, as a young man, being the King's chaplain, he had taken a message from Richmond to the Emperor in Flanders and brought back the answer to the King within the space of four days: this earned him promotion, first to be Dean of Lincoln and then Almoner, after which he never looked back.

While it was also desirable that a good postal service should exist for commercial purposes, so that merchants could enrich themselves and thus provide a more tempting prey for the tax collector, the public post was more prized by both Shakespeare's sovereigns, as an abundant source of material for the central intelligence service. There was no nonsense about respecting the privacy of the subjects' mail. The greater the personage, the more desirable it was for the monarchy that his communications should be sent by the public post, thus allowing the ubiquitous Mr Secretary a glimpse of them now and again. One never knew what the rebellious dog would be up to next.

But we are not concerned *only* with life at this exalted level in the real England between 1589 and 1613, any more than Shakespeare in his plays is concerned *only* with the activities of people out of the top drawer. And therefore we shall examine all the means by which people of all classes moved about the country, and by which their goods and merchandise also moved; and how this traffic is portrayed in the plays.

England at this time was not predominantly horse-borne but ox-drawn. There was no county in which the agricultural draught-ox was unknown; there were few in which plough-horses were more numerous than plough-oxen. In those counties where farm wagons, as opposed to carts, were in use, it was an axiom that if the plough was drawn by oxen so also was the wagon; but this was not nearly so absolute in the case of carts, which were more commonly drawn by horses even in ox-plough country. The ox-cart existed but was becoming rarer in Britain, more

Plough-horse on land unsuitable for oxen. The landscape is not realistic but the plough gear is.
Detail from Breughel, *The Fall of Icarus*, painted after 1560. (Musées Royaux des Beaux-Arts,
Brussels. Photograph: Picture Archive, Marburg)

and more restricted to the western and northern periphery, the Highland zone. In
general, this was the situation all over western Europe at the time, but it was a time
when England did not rank high in the European pecking-order of efficient land
travel. The contrast between sea and land in this respect was marked. The English

mariner was skilful, hardy and bold, not least in his ability to stomach the revolting victuals provided in royal and merchant ships alike. The English standard of pilotage and navigation was high, the ships well designed, embodying all the innovations of recent years, no matter where they were invented (a high proportion were of Dutch origin). Ships were well and soundly built of good material, well sparred and rigged. Their canvas was of good quality, and their cannon, cast of Sussex iron, shot truer than most contemporary pieces – as seamen of all nations ruefully acknowledged.

In transport by land, on the other hand, there was no field in which the English were pre-eminent and few in which they ranked even second-best. Perhaps the English post, as an organisation, enjoyed a respectable international status, but in terms of performance it lagged far behind what some Continental mail systems daily achieved. This was due to the design and upkeep of the road system which, it is true, suffered from the effects of a rainfall and general humidity with which few Continental road-builders had to contend. There were also European countries in which long-distance travel by coach was a commonplace, while in England it was no such thing (see Chapters 4 and 6 below). There were no English-built coaches, and the design and workmanship of English carts and wagons was not such as to excite the admiration of foreign visitors. The English packhorse system of commercial traffic was as well organised as any of its foreign counterparts, but there were other countries where – at any rate for commercial purposes – packhorse traffic was rather old hat.

In our modern age of mechanical transport we live in the afterglow of an era in which English horseflesh was the wonder and the envy of the western world. Shakespeare's England had no international prestige of this order. General utility horses in England struck the Continental visitor as being useful sorts, well up to the standard of the mainland for the same class of animal. English palfreys, the usual comfortable travelling conveyance throughout the country, were good; but, the visitor from abroad would reflect, so they had better be, because on these appalling roads travel by passenger carriage was not a practical proposition. Even so, the English palfrey was not quite of the same quality as the Spanish or Irish equivalent.

Of horses for higher ranks of society, the English really had none, home-bred. The English Great Horse, the mount of the gentleman in his capacity as knight or man-at-arms, was very much like its counterpart elsewhere in northwest Europe between, say, Brittany and Jutland, except that it shared with the Friesian, the breed which had contributed most to its make-up, a lack of speed and an even more dangerous lack, for campaigning purposes, of endurance. English military technique by land was conservative; more modern cavalry tactics demanded

Officer's charger, showing no trace of Spanish or Mediterranean influence in breeding, such as appeared later in the century. Hans Baldung, *St Martin of Tours Dividing his Cloak with the Beggar*, 1533. (Reproduced by courtesy of the Trustees of the British Museum)

something faster with more stamina for prolonged engagements. For the other functions for which the governing class required the Great Horse, 'state' or processional purposes and to display the skill of the rider in the art of manège, something more elegant and much handier was required. In England, the best and hence the most expensive horses were still the imported ones.

English equitation in that day contained no element not common to that of neighbouring countries, and as in the rest of Europe it fell into two categories: the

'A citizen riding with his wife.' (The British Library, EG. 1269)

civil and the military. The latter had during the past century thrown out a side-branch, the 'manage' – the art of equitation *per se*, school-riding. A form of this is still widely practised both in England and on the Continent and will have been seen at some time or other by practically everyone who has also seen a Shakespearian play, so no more need be said about it at the outset of this book.

On the other hand, because the alternative, the older civilian style of riding, is no longer practised anywhere in England today, but only in some overseas corners of the English-speaking world, more must be said about it. The military style which depended on the use of stirrups was essentially a creation of the age of chivalry, and the very earliest date at which it can have been practised is the reign of Charlemagne. But 'snaffle-riding' on the easy-going palfrey was invented long before the use of the stirrup, which it did not positively demand, though the presence of stirrups was no impediment to it. The horse never trotted: instead it either racked or ambled or paced. The rack is a rather spectacular gait in which the feet come to the ground not in diagonal pairs, but one by one all round the horse. The amble differs from the pace only in being slower; in both, the fore- and hind-feet move forward on the same side at once, causing a swaying motion like that of a camel. Horses so trained never galloped – they simply moved forward using their legs in the same sequence but faster and faster. The effect of both rack and pace was to give a much smoother ride at all speeds. It was eminently suitable for the pastime of hunting and hawking, as also for accommodating a lady on the pillion behind her cavalier.

3

Horse-breeding and the
horse in husbandry

The distinction between 'hard-going' and 'soft-going' horses was so important that the reader must not be surprised to find it treated at considerable length, and under different heads, hereinafter. Trotting saddle horses at this time were still a minority and to a certain extent a novelty. For the latter reason they figure more prominently in the up-to-date technical literature of the period, and also because the use of 'soft-going' horses was so much longer established, and their breeding so widespread, that few writers thought it necessary to give directions how to 'make' them, since this was a built-in part of the traditional horse-rearing lore.

The perfect palfrey was produced by a combination of breeding and training. But the latter began so early in life that it fell inevitably to the lot of the breeder to encourage the 'soft' lateral gait of the pace or amble. One of the few authors who tells us how it was done is Nicholas Morgan, a 'gentleman of ... the county of Kent'. Chapter 47 of his now little-known *Perfection of Horsemanship* (1609) is entitled 'The Manner to Teach a Colt to Amble Without Handling':

> You are to begin the lesson the next day after the [colt] is foaled. Put on a halter on the mare's head: in the morning early lead her forth, let the colt follow her so gently and soft pace as she can go, into some even, plain and hard ground, and be sure that the colt be not enforced to go faster than you lead the mare, and then observe and you shall find the colt going by her that he doth altogether go and train his legs in an amble. Thus continue leading the mare in soft and slow going about halfe an houre, and the colt will not himself go faster than his dam.

This is to be repeated again at midday, and again at six in the evening, and to continue for ten days.

and as the colt increaseth in swiftness of pace in his amble, so increase the pace of the mare, and he will amble most swiftly and perfectly: if you begin with that maner aforesaid, and never enforce him to go faster, use will bring him unto all perfection.

But even here so much is assumed to be common knowledge that it is not spelt out, and will escape the modern reader. It is taken for granted that the mare is a pacing mare, that her 'walk' or 'bottom gear' is an amble, right fore and right hind together and vice versa, and that the only hope of producing pacing foals was out of such a mare. The use of a pacing sire might or might not enhance that expectation, but would not by any means double it, as Morgan and other authorities (Thomas Blundeville, for instance) knew by experience. Morgan's method rests on recognition of the fact that a *tendency* to pace may be inherited genetically, as we would say, but the actual *doing* of it depends on the foal's imitating his dam's way of going. The instinct of the foal is to follow the mare, not to run in front of her, and this can be left to nature. Where art comes in is in the keeping of the mare's stride down to a length which the foal's little legs can compass; for if he has to hurry to keep up with her he may break into a trot, or a tripple, or a canter, so that the benefit of what students of animal behaviour now call 'imprinting' will be lost.

If it was lost, from this or any other cause, then later in life other means must be adopted to teach the pace and the amble. They demanded special equipment, time and labour, and hence money, and they are described by W. Browne in *Browne His Fiftie Yeares Practice* (1624). Those fifty years' practical experience had begun, on William Browne's part, in 1574, but this book embodies centuries of practical experience in traditional 'snaffle-riding, for trotting *and ambling* of all manner of horses whatsoever', and it represents the medieval technique of 'making' rather than breaking horses to the saddle, as also the Renaissance and early modern English system for all purposes except the highly specialised one of training the Great Horse. This demanded the use of the ferocious curb bit seen in illustrations to authors such as Blundeville, whereas the everyday riding for which Browne prepared them was done with a snaffle, looking, in Browne's illustrations, very much like those in use today. The training of harness horses plays no part in Browne's book, or Blundeville's or Morgan's, simply because the use of horses in harness was so restricted. Carriages, owned only by the very rich, were drawn by Great Horses, and probably by such as had proved not very satisfactory under the saddle; thus they were already broken when they first came between the traces, and such specialised training as they got was effected by yoking them together with horses that had already worked in a harness team. Therefore there is no book on harness training as such at this period. Browne's methods are still practised today in various parts of the English-speaking world, but such is the mutability of

Mouthing the young horse, illustration to Browne, *His Fiftie Yeares Practice*. (The British Library)

equine fortunes that they are practised now in different sectors of the sphere of light harness driving.

Of William Browne's life we know nothing save that he was born in or about 1554, and he describes himself as 'an old northern man' (but 'Gentleman' on the title page). This in itself is significant. In the first place, in and before the time of William Browne's birth the reputation of the North Country for light saddle horses had been paramount in England and was still considerable in James I's time. Secondly, it is principally in Yorkshire and Lancashire, in Cumbria and Durham, that the legitimate heirs of the Browne tradition still practise today. There, horses are still occasionally taught to pace, for sulky racing purposes, by the use of hobbles or lateral couplings called locally in his day 'side-lanyells'; and for trotting racing they are made to develop a high action, as show hackneys are, by attaching weights to the feet. However, nowadays this is done by the use of extra-heavy shoes, and not, as Browne advocates, with wooden spheres of about six inches in diameter, tied to the pasterns so as to fit in the hollow between the heel and the fetlock. In Durham I have actually seen a combination of Browne's and Morgan's principles still applied, at a show of Dales ponies. The class was for mares with foals at foot, and the presumption was that the foals would grow up to

Lungeing, illustration to Browne, *His Fiftie Yeares Practice*. (The British Library)

become outstanding trotters, in harness. One of them was shod, at less than three months old. I was so surprised that I rather naively asked the owner what the shoes were for. He replied, dead-pan, 'Well, it saves their feet, doesn't it?' Of course a foal running at pasture with the mare does not need its feet 'saving'. The real purpose of those shoes was to teach the foal at the earliest possible age (Morgan) to develop a 'loftie trot' (Browne) by artificially weighting the feet.

When a horse had graduated from the Browne school as 'perfit both for the trot and amble' then it was known as 'pac'd' or 'thorough-pac'd', and in a later chapter we shall see how Shakespeare employed these terms. A good horse of this class (which by modern standards we should rate a pony) fetched £40 or £50. Pending another round in the spiral of inflation, this would be £800 to £1000 of modern money.

Details of the actual practice of horse-breeding, which was governed by tradi-tional lore and the accumulated experience of past generations, are sparsely recorded in print. It is in general only the theorists who publish at this period, and innovators like Blundeville who tell us something in translation of the methods of foreign breeders like the Italians, some of which they are seeking to introduce.

Such a theorist is Nicholas Morgan, from whom we learn something about

Title page from Browne, *His Fiftie Yeares Practice*. It is possible that the illustration was selected by the printer from his stock of cuts without the author's approval, and that it does not represent the author himself. Browne was an expert on 'snaffle riding', whereas this horse is plainly wearing a curb. (The British Library)

English practice in that part of his *Perfection of Horsemanship* in which he differs from the custom of his countrymen. For instance, on the question of when to cover the mare, he tells us that most horsemasters did so in March or April or May, adding that they did this in order to have foals born at the season when the spring grass was most abundant. However, he believed that the period of gestation was a year and ten days, although generations of observation on the part of studmasters must have established the fact that it is really round about 333 days. If his figures were right, the desired effect would still not be obtained. The traditional date for turning stock out to grass was Helenmass (during the first week of May). A mare covered at the end of March would foal down, according to the Morgan schedule, about April 10, when there is often still no flush of grass at all, even in Kent where Morgan lived, let alone in the North Country which in his time was the best breeding ground for horses in England. But, reckoning by the real period of gestation, she would be more likely to foal about 28 February, in the bleakest season of the year. Not that he cares, because in any case he is not in favour of keeping mares with sucking foals at grass, since he considers the milk of grass-fed mares to be thin and waterish. Of course it is, as is the milk of all mares – it is 'blue' no matter how the mare is fed. The fat content is low, the sugar content high, and that is what suits foals. But Morgan, and some other theorists of the day, judged all milk by the standard of cows' milk, and much of his advice on the subject of foaling and the care of sucking foals is intended to give the milk a bovine look. Fortunately for English horse-breeding these views did not prevail.

In fact, covering mares in March or earlier was no doubt much less common then than it is now, because the prime motive for this action arises, almost exclusively, in Thoroughbred circles from the practice of racing two-year-olds and the consequent desire for the colts to be as old as possible when they go into training in the second year of their lives. But Shakespeare lived and died a century before the genesis of the Thoroughbred, and Elizabethan racing men were willing to take their time about entering horses to the racing game. 'Do not make a courser [racehorse] of him', says the old northern man William Browne, 'till he be six or seven yeare olde.' By this time the track career of the modern racehorse is usually over.

Lord Willoughby, writing to Robert Cecil on 16 May 1600, points out 'My old mares being at this tyme of yeare so greet with foale' – and the majority of studs would be in the same situation at that season. Most breeders, then as now, would go on covering mares right into the late summer if they had not managed to get them in foal before that, and they had an additional reason for doing so which motivates few breeders today. Many breeders then believed firmly that sex deter-mination was possible, and could be arranged by letting the mare conceive under a female sign of the zodiac if filly foals were wanted, or a male sign if a colt was desired. As the signs in the three spring months are Aries, Taurus and Gemini, only colts could be expected from a mating under them. The only safe way to get a filly was to cover under the sign of Virgo, for which one would have to wait until late August: it would be possible also in September (Libra); but otherwise it was very difficult for a breeder to 'have a mare-colt at your pleasure', as William Browne says, because all the other feminine signs fall in the winter time, when mares are least likely to come in season. Indeed one wonders how the female equine population was kept up at all in the face of this astrological handicap.

'Teasers' were in use to test whether the mares were in season, at least in the more expensive establishments, to save the wear and tear on the stallion's nervous system. Morgan recommends the use of a 'little ston'd jade' to try mares with.*

Although horse-breeding in Shakespeare's England was a matter of private enterprise, those landowners who were not considered enterprising enough in this matter were prodded onwards by the state. Government policy in this respect, as in all the countries of the western world, was conditioned by the requirements of the Army Remounts Department in various guises, and had been so throughout the Middle Ages and was to continue so far into the internal combustion age. England down to the reign of Henry VII had had much the same pattern of horse-breeding for military purposes as, say, France. Essentially this was a system initiated by Edward I, having for its objects first the provision of Great Horses, armour-carrying equine juggernauts that were a weapon in themselves, and secondly other horses 'for service in the wars' but suitable for light cavalry – 'half-armed men' – and mounted archers (see below, Chapter 14). Under the Edwardian system the breeding of large warhorses (destriers) was a Crown-owned, Crown-run enterprise. Every royal castle was in the charge of a constable, whose duties included the upkeep of a stud of brood mares (on average about two dozen) in the castle grounds. These were served by stallions, also the property of the Crown, which rotated from castle to castle every few seasons, often over long distances. Thus stallions from Merton in Surrey and Tutbury in Staffordshire are recorded as having stood certain seasons in Edward II's reign at Pickering in Yorkshire.

Light horses for military use were obtained from among those bred by husbandmen, almost entirely on the common grazing. When Shakespeare first came to London it was a hundred years since the last real full-scale battle between mounted men-at-arms, armour against armour, had been fought on English soil, and the wars in France with their avid demands for horseflesh had been less frequent during the sixteenth century than in any previous one since the times of William I. The hiring of foreign (usually German) mercenaries, complete with 'High Almain' troop-horses, had become frequent during the reigns of Henry VII and his son, and by 1536 this network of royal studs of horses 'fit for service in the wars' had more holes than cord in it. But the grandiose and unrealistic ambitions of Henry VIII to play a leading warlike part on the European stage led him to try to rebuild the

---

* This expression is frequently misunderstood today; whereas stoned cherries have the stones out, stoned colts have the stones in. Quality is irrelevant so a jade will do.

Colt-herd with youngstock. Woodcut from Fugger, *Von der Gestüterey*, 1584. (Reproduced by permission of Miland Publishers, Nieuwkoop, Netherlands)

Edwardian structure by a new and characteristically Tudor device of delegating responsibility and expense. All persons of a certain 'estate', spiritual as well as temporal, were required to keep stallions suitable for military heavy remount breeding; dukes and archbishops had to maintain eight, and the scale went down to private persons with a certain annual income, who had to keep one. Brood mares were required to be kept, so many per mile of perimeter, by all gentlemen who empaled parks for deer (see Chapter 13 below) and minimum standards of size were laid down for these mares. In both cases penalties took the form of very stiff fines; but compliance seems to have been exceptional since throughout the reigns of Edward VI, Mary and Elizabeth the relevant laws were frequently re-enacted, the preamble, each time, fulminating against the slackness of those subjects on whom this patriotic duty was laid. All these laws were still on the statute book throughout the lifetime of William Shakespeare. So were other laws requiring certain minimum standards in horses (in effect, ponies) kept for breeding purposes on the common grazings. Thus in the last quarter of the sixteenth century, broadly speaking, the better sorts of horse or pony for all purposes were being bred in parks, the cheaper sorts on commons, heaths, moors and fens.

There had for a long time been a great under-estimation of the sexual power of the stallion and its relation to his physical capacity in general. It was still unthinkable, as it had been in the Middle Ages, to demand any sort of work from a horse during the mating season, and the number of mares which a stallion was

expected to cover in one season was as ludicrously small as it had been in Edward
II's time. This attitude is well summed up by Nicholas Morgan, in Chapter 58 on
the causes of long life:

> The fift cause of long life is to keepe a horse from the excessive spending himselfe
> upon mares, for its death's best harbinger, for it wasteth the spirits, weakeneth the
> stomacke, and dryeth up the brains, and marrowe, and therefore the reason why a
> Mule, being a mixed creature, begotten between a Horse and an Asse, is longer liued
> then either of them, is for that his lusting in that kind is but once onlie in the whole
> course of his life.

The proportion of entire horses of all breeds to the total number of equines was
far higher throughout the country than it is today, and this made selective breeding
far more difficult, since the possibility of an undesirable mating lay round every
corner. The reason for this excess of stallions lay in a lingering relic, again, of a
common medieval attitude: in upper-class circles it was unthinkable for a
gentleman to ride a mare, and the English being such snobs as they were and are,
hardly anybody who aspired to ride wanted to ride a mare, and few men would be
content with a gelding either. Probably this attitude had its roots in the far past of
pre-Christian religious concepts associating the stallion with sexual prowess and
fertility in general, making it the only proper mount for a man. But this attitude
had been weakening ever since the times of Henry VII, when the practice of
castration ('libbing') became much more general among horses for town use,
although it made less headway against rural conservatism. However, among the
more sophisticated layers of society the gelding as a mount for everyday occasions,
though not those of 'state', was gaining ground.

This was much more clearly the case with horses for ladies. As the jailer's
daughter sings in the not wholly Shakespearian *Two Noble Kinsmen*:*

> He's buy me a white cut, forth for to ride.   (III, iv, 22)

Some glossators maintain that 'cut' here means a horse with a docked tail, and
there may be instances where this is so, but the many contexts where Cut is the
name of a packhorse, which would be at a disadvantage without a complete tail,
and a nuisance if entire, tend to show that the word more frequently meant
gelding. The more expensive geldings were imports from Hungary and Bohemia,
the cheaper ones from the Scottish lowlands. For what it is worth, the form 'he's'
for 'he shall' is a Northernism, of a kind that Shakespeare never attempted
elsewhere (though Ben Jonson did in *Bartholomew Fair*, for example).

An inventory of horses in the Queen's stables, made in October 1598 and
appearing among the Cecil papers, lists twenty-two geldings, two of which are for

* This play, printed in 1634, is believed to be the work of Shakespeare and John Fletcher.

the Queen's personal use and the other twenty for her ladies-in-waiting. At the foot of the same list are added 'two coults of four & five year old'; indicative of the sensibly unhurried tempo of horse breeding in that day. They were still called colts at five, and their presence in this particular list seems to indicate that in due course they might be castrated and put to the same use as the other geldings. Whereas nowadays it is exceptional to perform this operation much after the age of two, it was then prudent to wait until maturity in order to be quite sure that the colt was not a late developer and might not after all prove suitable for one of the proper employments of an entire horse (war, for instance).

The simple solution of castration had never been widely practised as at least a negative aid to better breeding (except, it seems, in Scotland and the North); it was only an increased demand for geldings to ride, and also for work in coach-teams, that led to more colts being cut and fewer sub-standard stallions being at large. But these beneficent side-effects can hardly have begun to operate to the improvement of English horse-breeding in the lifetime of William Shakespeare.

ဩ ဩ ဩ

The work which first brought Shakespeare public acclaim not only contains, line for line, a greater density of equestrian allusions than any other single work of Shakespeare's, it also contains two spectacular passages connected with horse-breeding. One of these, examined in detail in Chapter 7, describes in orthodox terms what has been taken to represent the Elizabethan ideal of equine conformation, and hence the type most aimed at by Elizabethan breeders; the other, less derivative and more likely to be the fruit of everyday observation by the boy from Warwickshire, paints realistically the sexual behaviour of the equine male. *Venus and Adonis* (1593) was probably Shakespeare's first published work, and immediately became a great hit.

Since for every dozen of our readers who are at all familiar with the plays there will not be more than one who has ever read a line of *Venus and Adonis*, here is a synopsis. It is a short story in verse, beginning as comedy and ending as tragedy; tragedy indeed of the antique pattern, culminating in the violent death of the young god. The only two characters are described in entirely human terms. Adonis is beautiful but dumb, a frigid and dedicated rider to hounds of a type familiar to us today, but currently more common in the feminine gender than the masculine (there is a sort of cycle in this – the sex ratio changes every few generations). Venus is – well, Venus at her earthiest. The only unearthly thing about her is her means of transport: a dove-propelled aerial chariot. She encounters this priggish little Pony Club graduate on his way to a meet of the Olympian Boarhounds – 'Hunting he lov'd, but love he laugh'd to scorn' (4) – and the opening is very nearly slapstick. She literally pulls him out of his saddle ('Vénus toute entière à sa proie attachée')* and with the reins over one arm and the great big beautiful doll under the other retires to a thicket, tying his hunter to 'a ragged bough' by the reins, exactly as the instructors tell us not to. For more than 220 lines she subjects Adonis to a process of vamping, but makes absolutely no headway. Their dialogue, or rather her monologue (for he is tongue-tied as well as everything else), is interrupted by the entry of 'a breeding jennet' which neighs at Adonis's hunter; he predictably breaks loose and 'to her straight goes'. Adonis unwisely attempts to catch his horse at this point; the mare takes fright and exits, pursued by stallion (most hunters in Shakespeare's day were entire), pursued, but not very far, by stallion's owner. Adonis may be stupid but not as stupid as to think he can run faster than a horse. While Adonis is getting his wind back, Venus attacks him strongly, along the lines that his horse is a better man than he is. She does, in this second round, strike some sparks from him, for at least she provokes him to utterance, and she detains him in argument far into the night; but only in argument. Off he goes, intending to hunt again on the morrow, in some part of the country not infested by wanton goddesses.

And now the whole atmosphere of the poem changes, and a chill wind blows through it, as Venus wanders through the forest in the pale dawn, seeking the hounds of Adonis and his companions, full of foreboding that the boar must be the death of him, 'For now she knows it is no gentle chase' (883) when she hears the pack baying at some quarry that will stand and face them. One after another she passes wounded hounds, and then the hunted boar, and then more hounds dying of those 'crooked tushes' (624). Lastly she comes on her unloving beloved, dead of the abdominal wounds that were the end of so many boar-hunters.

There is a line here, near the beginning of the poem, that is almost a stock-breeder's maxim:

> Seeds spring from seeds, and beauty breedeth beauty   (167)

There is no practical studmaster nor theoretical geneticist who would quarrel with that today. And shortly after, there appears a line that to the modern ear sounds an absolute contradiction in terms:

> A breeding jennet, lusty, young and proud   (260)

In British English of the twentieth century a jennet is the same as a hinny, the hybrid progeny of a stallion and a she-ass, and like the mule invariably sterile: it cannot breed in our sense of the word. In modern American ears the line is not so

---

* 'Venus herself grasping her prey' (Racine, *Phèdre* II.v.304).

nonsensical; to Americans, breeding means not so much parturition as copulation of which the hinny is perfectly capable. And in America, a jennet is a she-ass (*anglice* jenny). But in the day of Shakespeare the word had not acquired either of these meanings. It was an anglicisation of the Spanish word *ginete*, originally meaning a pacing pony, usually one bred in the northwest of Spain – Asturias or Galicia. By this time it had come to be applied to the full-sized Iberian warhorse. 'Proud' in this context means on heat; 'pride' is still used as a synonym for oestrus by some horsemasters today.

The text-book description of the perfect horse (see Chapter 7) comes between two passages that describe in detail the courting display of the stallion in the presence of mares which he knows – or hopes – are in season (265–88 and 301–18). This is quite different from the intimidating rivalry-display provoked by the sight or scent of another stallion, and all its salient features are described, from:

> His ears up-prick'd, his braided hanging mane
> Upon his compass'd crest now stand on end;
> His nostrils drink the air, and forth again
> As from a furnace, vapours doth he send ...
> Sometime he trots, as if he told the steps,
> With gentle majesty and modest pride;
> Anon he rears upright, curvets and leaps   (271–9)

to:

> Sometimes he scuds far off, and there he stares;
> Anon he starts at stirring of a feather;
> To bid the wind a base he now prepares,
> And where he run or fly, they know not whether,
> For through his mane and tail the high wind sings,
> Fanning the hairs, who wave like feather'd wings.
>
> He looks upon his love, and neighs unto her: ...
> She puts on outward strangeness, seems unkind,
> Spurns at his love, and scorns the heat he feels,
> Beating his kind embracements with her heels ...   (301–12)

A great deal of the effort put into horsemanship in Shakespeare's day was intended, as now, to show the horse to the best advantage, though not for quite the same social reasons, as we shall see in Chapter 7. But there was and is no artifice or exercise that the human exhibitor can contrive to equal in effectiveness the show put on spontaneously by the stallion on free range in the presence of mares.

The likeliest place to observe this spectacle, *then*, was a deer-park; the number of such parks throughout the country reached its peak early in the reign of James I. All governments since the time of Henry VIII had been willing to tolerate the waste

'Beating his kind embracements with her heels.' Woodcut from Fugger, *Von der Gestüterey*, 1584. (Reproduced by permission of Miland Publishers, Nieuwkoop, Netherlands)

of good agricultural land so used, and about which writers on rural economy complained, by the laws mentioned above binding every gentleman 'empaling' such a park to provide and keep in it at his own expense brood mares suitable for breeding cavalry remounts, the number in proportion to the park's 'compass' or perimeter. They were to be served by the stallions which certain persons of rank or of a certain income were also legally obliged to provide and keep at their own charges. It was a neat system, which never worked as intended, but could be observed in action in any of the deer-parks with which Warwickshire was so amply provided (all marked on Robert Morden's map of that county). There is a widely honoured tradition, even if documentary evidence is lacking, that the young Shakespeare was a great frequenter of deer-parks, not entirely for legitimate purposes.

One other point, at the far end of the breeder's activities, where they shade off into those of the trainer, is very succinctly dealt with in *Venus and Adonis*, and the two lines are perhaps more relevant to our own day than to the age in which they were written:

> The colt that's back'd and burden'd being young,
> Loseth his pride, and never waxeth strong.   (419–20)

Premature breaking and working of young horses, in most societies, is the result of an overall shortage. Given the ample stocks, in quantity if not in quality, available in Elizabeth I's England, this harmful practice is unlikely to have been widespread. Certainly there were no races for two-year-old colts and fillies in those days. The 'breeding jennet' of this poem is sexually mature but 'unbacked', and might very well remain so all her life. The proportion of all mares to be reserved for breeding only was higher in relation to the total horse population then than now. This was partly the result of social convention, with the lingering and half-conscious prejudice among persons of rank against riding mares; and for this purpose 'rank' extended a long way down the scale. The commonest employment for mares was either in harness (but not to coaches) or in the pack-train, but as we have seen a great deal of slow harness work was a closed shop for horses anyway – only oxen need apply. The mare had a well-defined function in the service of the carrier, but of its very nature it limited the numbers employed. Every pack-train was made up of a bell-mare, who took the lead, having attached to her pack-saddle a spherical brass bell, and anything up to nine geldings who did not have to be led or driven, but followed the mare wherever she went by day or night, in clear weather or in fog, just as long as they could hear the bell. If all carriers had run to the full establishment of ten horses (each carrying 2 cwt and thus a ton between them) there would not have been so many mares in the carrying trade. But there was, all over the country, a host of small undertakings running not more than half a dozen packhorses, but each needing a bell-mare, and so the proportion was kept up.

The practice of breeding from mares whose own performance was untried does not seem to have raised doubts in the minds of breeders at any level, outside the still very restricted circle of racehorse breeders. So far as park-bred jennets are concerned I have seen only one instance (in 1600) in which a filly of this type, offered by Lord Willoughby to the Marquis of Salisbury to run as a brood mare in Hatfield Park, is described as 'rightly bred by sire *and dam*'. Both contemporary medical theory and popular tradition regarded the role of the sexes in reproduction in a very unequal light. The uterus was looked on as little more than a hothouse, the existence of the ovum was barely guessed at, and the nature of the sperm not fully understood. To use human terms, each spermatozoon was regarded as a 'homunculus' – a tiny little man – and all the mother did for it, pre-natally, was to provide facilities for it to grow and grow and grow. What we understand as fertilisation the best scientific brains of Shakespeare's generation looked on as more in the nature of implantation. Therefore a practical demonstration of the mare's ability to 'draw' or to 'run' herself was not a factor in selecting her for breeding. Here the criterion was rather which mare will provide the best possible pre-natal conditions for the 'equunculus' – the foal which is already formed in its sire's image, on a microscopic scale, at the moment of conception. And before you scoff at this belief, remember there *were* no microscopes. 'Seeds grow from seeds' was taken very literally, the seeds proceeding entirely from the male ancestry. Some lingering echo of this view of the function of the sexes in heredity is heard in the synonym for uterus – 'foal-*bed*' – still current in some rural dialects today. Not so much a bed of feathers as a bed of roses or radishes.

In this as in other matters, Shakespeare was bound by the limits but also shared fully the capacity of 'natural philosophy' in our country and that age. 'Which like the toad, ugly and venomous,/Wears yet a precious jewel in his head' (*As You Like It* II, i, 13) is to us pernicious nonsense – we *know* toads are not poisonous (even though some people get inflamed hands after handling toads), we *know* they do not have jewels in their heads, because we have been nourished on the fruits of experimental biology since the days of Darwin and Huxley. But it was not *our* experiment. We take for granted what the wise men tell us, though in our grandchildren's time their wisdom may be utterly refuted. What we see in a horse, and what Shakespeare saw, are identical. It is only what he and we read that is different. And what he saw and read he fused and transmuted into verse of imperishable grandeur, whereas we—

THE HORSE IN HUSBANDRY

Since the majority of horses in Shakespeare's time were bred by farmers of one sort or another, it is pertinent to enquire what use the husbandman and yeomen made of those they did not sell. This varied in different parts of the country. As we have seen in Chapter 2, horse ploughing was not at all common in the Warwickshire of Shakespeare's youth, though at the time he came to London it was well established in the region to the northeast of the capital, stretching away through Essex and Cambridgeshire into East Anglia. But even in this region much depended on the nature of the soil. In dryer ground, and on light or sandy soils, horse ploughing (without the use of horseshoes) was the rule, but in the low country, especially on heavy clays, oxen were unchallenged. What animal was used in the plough decided also what would be used in the wagon.

Regardless of the nature of soil, however, harrowing was always done by horses. Carting, as opposed to wagon-work, was also done by horses. But the use of wheeled vehicles was so restricted that all farm horses were dual purpose. That is, they were used either in the cart or under the pack-saddle. And their most frequent employment was still what it had been in Chaucer's day: carrying sacks of corn to the mill and meal away from it, and pack-loads of various produce to the weekly market. A further use, not restricted to farmers, was as the motive power of various kinds of mills, presses and water-raising devices, specially where for topographical reasons waterpower and windpower were not available. The horses worked either a capstan or a treadmill.

That only the worst of the horses they bred were commonly kept by farmers for their own use appears from their price in relation to draught-oxen. Admittedly the latter is enhanced by the fact that a seven-year-old draught-ox was edible, whereas worn-out work-horses were not so, by English standards. The carthorse of the period was worth about £2 10s at most. The answer to the question in *II Henry IV* (1598) 'How a good yoke of bullocks at Stamford fair?' (III, ii, 37) is answered by an entry in the Cecil household accounts for 1610. The Cecils' steward, Mr Bussey, paid £10 for a yoke of oxen at Stamford.

As well as in East Anglia, horses ploughed mainly in the North and the far West, on steep slopes where oxen were at a disadvantage, and these regions were beyond the practical horizon of William Shakespeare. So that he is not thinking merely of classical tradition where he speaks of oxen yoked in the plough: 'as the ox hath his bow' (*As You Like It* III, iii, 71) which kept the yoke in place.

Wagons, for reasons stated above, were as often drawn by oxen as by horses, except for the new-style wagons coming into use then among the more progressive wholesalers in the wool and textile trades. For the cart, exclusively drawn by horses, there were two methods of harnessing if more than one horse was in draught. The older method was with a pair, one either side of the draught-pole, which was a straightforward adaptation of the ox-pair with its single yoke. The newer method involved the use of shafts, as for a single horse – a 'fill-horse' as in *The Merchant of Venice* (II, ii, 91). Thill is a word for shaft still used in some parts of England, and *fill* probably a Londonism, since the Cockneys still say *frough fick and fin*. To this could be added a 'forehorse', drawing in traces, as in *All's Well That Ends Well* (II, i, 30). The expression 'forehorse' is still in use where this method of harnessing is customary, notably in Suffolk. When the team was decorated on festive occasions the forehorse was the more elaborately dressed of the two; and this is the most common significance when 'forehorse' is used figuratively.

As to the breaking of horses by farmer-breeders before sale, there is an allusion to this elementary stage of equine education in *Midsummer Night's Dream*, where Lysander says:

> He hath rid his prologue like a rough colt; he knows not the stop.
>
> (V, i, 119)

Horses bred on extensive common grazing were always marked in one of two ways to signify ownership: either by branding or by a system of ear-marking which provided more means of identification than one would think, by various combinations of slitting, cropping and piercing one or both ears. To this Hotspur refers when he says, in *I Henry IV*:

> What horse? A roan, a crop-ear is it not?   (II, iii, 70)

One cannot help but be struck, reading accounts of medieval horse breeding and those of the sixteenth centuries, by the difference in feeding scales between that accorded the brood mare and the stallion. The mare hardly ever gets anything but hay until after she has foaled, while the stallion is crammed with as much oats as the owner can afford. While it is true that mares which are too fat do not conceive as readily as those that are on the slender side, it is equally true that obesity in the stallion is no aid to fertility. In the wild state the stallion is literally 'fighting fit' in the breeding season, since he has had to battle for possession of his mares against other males. But it seems to have been the aim of the old-time studmaster to reverse this natural state of affairs. This matter also came under Shakespeare's observation, since he makes King Lear say: 'the soiled horse goes to it' (IV, vi, 124), and soiled means overfed.

4

Travelling

THE POST

The English postal system of the period was rather below the average of efficiency for western Europe, but within living memory it had been much worse. As late as 1533 the only regular public post in all England had been that between London and Dover. But in the early 1590s, when *Love's Labour's Lost* was first performed, a great reform took place in the carrying of mail to the Continent from England. Hitherto there had been three different and competing postal systems for foreign letters (including those circular letters from German and Low Country commercial correspondents that took the place of newspapers). There had been the Strangers' Post, organised by the foreign commercial community in London – the Flemings, the Dutch and the German Merchants of the Steelyard – and the Adventurers' Post, run by their opposite numbers, the English merchants resident abroad in such towns as the Channel Ports and the inland commercial cities of Flanders: these latter, or rather the people who put up the money for them, were known as Merchant Adventurers, not because they ever put their lives in hazard in the course of trade, but because they risked their capital. This is a common use of the word in Shakespeare, as in:

> I should adventure for such merchandise.   (*Romeo and Juliet*, II, ii, 84)

Lastly, there was the Queen's Post, which also functioned internally in the realm, to Ireland and as far as the Scottish border.

All were subject to some measure of censorship and outside interference. All, on English territory, were liable to be opened by agents of the secret police run by Sir

Woodcut illustrating the title page of Nicholas Breton, *A Post with a Pacquet of Mad Letters*, published in the seventeenth century. (By permission of the Syndics of Cambridge University Library)

Francis Walsingham, but especially letters sent by the Queen's Post, within which organisation he had his men permanently planted. Mail in the Strangers' and Adventurers' Posts might be opened and scrutinised by the intelligence agents of the foreign powers concerned, and it was suspected by English businessmen that those who ran the Strangers' Post were not above unfairly delaying the transit of a letter to or from an English firm if thereby some German or Flemish competitor could get the business arising out of it. This was about the only reason a London merchant would have for using the royal post which was at least only subject to political censorship. In any case, after 1591 he no longer had the option.

Internally, the fastest time made by the royal post was from London to Dover or return – twelve hours or five miles in the hour by 1600. But to recall Wolsey's exploits as a young chaplain at the beginning of the century (Chapter 2), as he was coming *back* along the Dover road from his record-breaking trip to Flanders he had met the royal post which had set out the same day as he did. Beyond London the rate was much slower. Letters from London to addresses in County Durham commonly took eight days. Post to the West Country took about as long, but performance was very uneven. Sometimes unexpected records were set up, under the right conditions of weather and long daylight, as when a post despatched from Plymouth on 25 July 1599 reached London by the 27th. Normally the post to, say, Taunton, took much longer than that to Retford which lay at the same distance from London, because beyond Retford, at the far end of the Great North Road, there lay, until 1603, the frontier of a foreign and potentially hostile power. The road to the west was only of importance to the government in so far as it was the road to the naval station at Plymouth, whose strategic importance varied from time to time with the foreign political situation; at times when the Spanish situation was more than usually threatening, special measures to improve West-Country communications were taken.

Within the period under review, the 'post' meant, to the Englishman in the theatre audience, a government-run service involving the use of ridden horses (no vehicles whatsoever) and intended primarily for the conveyance of official messages. Two-horse post-chaises had existed in Roman Britain and were to appear again in the England of the Georges. But to Shakespeare's contemporaries there was no such thing as a post on wheels. But the post-horses were also, and increasingly, available on a fee-paying basis for private correspondence and passengers. By definition beyond the scope of this book, but worth noting *en passant*, there was also a foot-post established for special purposes where the roads were more than usually unsuitable for horsed traffic, or in special crises like that of the Spanish Armada of 1588. Both the Crown and some powerful nobles still maintained private couriers for the dispatch of specially urgent messages, and some of these were literally 'runners'; carrying messages was the duty of the Running Footman on the establishment of a few great houses, and his dis-advantage *vis-à-vis* the mounted courier lay not at all in the distance he could cover in a given time – he was not like the horseman confined to the road – but in the limits to the weight he could carry. But what complicated the postal admin-istration sometimes beyond measure was the legitimate practice of hiring the post-horses to people with valid warrants for purposes of travel, for which they paid twopence a mile to 'ride post'. It was this taking-up of the post-horses that was responsible for most postal delays.

Because under certain circumstances postmasters were empowered to impress horses if those at their disposal were disabled or unfit for work (every postmaster kept a minimum of three), a warrant of April 1596 commanded a list of owners of available horses to be made for every township throughout the country, and thus though the human population had no census taken in Shakespeare's time, there was, throughout the greater part of his dramatic career, a complete census of English working horses.

The word 'post' occurs with great frequency throughout Shakespeare's works: noun and verb some sixty-five times by my count, besides two *postmasters*, five *post-hastes* and three *post-horses*. Divination by tape-measure is abhorrent, but a statistic like this cannot be ignored. Upwards of seventy-five instances show that the post, as an institution, had become an ever-present part of the lives of ordinary middle-class Englishmen, which it certainly had not been in the time of the Queen's late father.

Thus in *King John* the Bastard Faulconbridge, speaking unwittingly of his wife, says:

> What woman-post is this? hath she no husband
> That will take pains to blow a horn before her?   (I, i, 218)

The horn was an essential part of the post-rider's equipment, since it was meant to warn beforehand all those people who had special duties to perform at every stage in speeding the post on his way. Hence its use in England and many other countries as an emblem of postal service.

Post-haste is a reference to the inscription commonly written on the outside of letters, below the address – 'Haste post haste, for thy life' – often reinforced by a crude drawing of a booted corpse dangling from the gallows. The penalty for dawdling on postal business was supposed to be death, but I do not know of a single instance of such a sentence being carried out.

Post-boys were notoriously an unprepossessing lot, and this is the point in *The Merry Wives of Windsor*, where the bogus Anne Page proves to be a postmaster's boy from Eton.

In *Coriolanus* the line

> Your native town you enter'd like a post,
> And had no welcomes...   (V, vi, 50)

vouches for the everyday familiarity of the post to English people. When the post-boy rides into town, blow his horn as he may, nobody even looks round.

INNS

Because of the horse-hiring business, the vocation of postmaster was inseparably connected with the innkeeping trade, and by the end of the century all towns and many villages on main roads had one inn among the other inns known as the Post House, and displaying, besides its own peculiar sign of the Angel or the Woolpack or the Garter, a post-horn in token of its special function.

It is notable among the accounts of those households which kept large numbers of horses that expenses on the hire of post-horses were high, and the rate charged was rising rapidly throughout the period. At the beginning it was about 2d a mile. By 1604 the Cecil household at Hatfield was paying 4½d a mile per horse, so that to send one man to Bath and back riding post from London would cost £4 in horse-hire alone.

If private horses were used, the inn's account for horse provender and attendance was about as much, for one horse, as for one rider (excluding his drink). It depended whether bread or oats were fed. The price of horsebread as paid to the brownbaker (see Chapter 16 below) was theoretically controlled at ½d a loaf throughout the period, and the quartern (4 lb) loaf was a feed for one horse. But the ostler's reckoning where bread was fed came to much more than the price of two horse-loaves. Where oats were fed the charge was about 5d a feed, and hay for one night about 4½d. Inn charges for horses hardly ever came to less than 1s 6d a night, which was a good deal more than a groom's daily wages. At this rate it would cost 6s a night to put up a team of four coach horses, even if no charge were made for 'parking' the coach.

A FAIR DAY'S MARCH

For a special journey whose route could be anticipated, a rich traveller would 'lay posts' – that is, send his own horses ahead along the way to be ready for him in relay stages. It was by this means that in 1603 Sir Robert Carey rode from Richmond, Surrey to Edinburgh in sixty-six hours, but this was an all-time record, and ample time for preparations had been afforded during the Queen's illness: the purpose of the journey being to announce her death, and his accession, to James I. The distance is about 406 miles, and the performance outstanding by Continental standards. A comparable distance of nearly 390 miles from Constantinople to a destination in Hungary was covered by an embassy to Transylvania in eight days in 1629, and reckoned good time.

Ordinary travellers on horseback seldom made more than about 30 miles a day, no more than they had done in Chaucer's time, and this would cost something like 7s 6d in post-horse hire.

| Imogen: | How many score of miles may we well ride |
| | 'Twixt hour, and hour? |

Palfrey and running footman. Woodcut from Fugger, *Von der Gestüterey*, 1584. (Reproduced by permission of Miland Publishers, Nieuwkoop, Netherlands)

Pisanio:	One score 'twixt sun and sun,
	Madam's enough for you; and too much too.
Imogen:	Why, one that rode to's execution, man,
	Could never go so slow: I have heard of riding wagers,
	Where horses have been nimbler than the sands
	That run i' th' clock's behalf...
	... provide me presently
	A riding-suit; no costlier than would fit
	A franklin's housewife. (*Cymbeline* III, ii, 68–78)

One curious result of Shakespeare's habit of placing historical characters in the setting of his own century is to slow down the pace of their movements. A real British lady of rank in the reign of the historical Cymbeline (Cunobelinus) would have rattled along in a chariot and pair like Boudicca, covering perhaps three score miles on one of the better tracks, like the Ridgeway, provided the weather were dry, between sunrise and sunset. Sixteen centuries later, things were different. The great increase in population, the far greater volume of traffic, the constant movement of great herds of livestock on the hoof converging from the North and

West on the marts of the more populous Southeast, had waged a war of attrition on the road system of the country. The roads had not had an effective system of maintenance, even on a local scale, since the Roman governmental machine had ground to a halt more than a thousand years before Shakespeare was born.

'Franklin' was becoming a rather old-fashioned term (it had been commoner in the mouths of Chaucer's characters than Shakespeare's), but it still meant a substantial agricultural freeholder, not exactly a gentleman – the sort of person who was coming more and more to be called a yeoman, and very different from the yeoman of Chaucer's time, who was an upper servant, someone's valet, like the Canon's Yeoman. Riding-suits in the wardrobe of such prosperous rural middle-class women would get most of their airing on necessary journeys, since riding for pleasure was more characteristic of the gentry's wives and daughters. Riding was still a useful accomplishment rather than a genteel 'extra', because there was simply no other acceptable method of transport available for women. The alternatives will be itemised below, but they were very few, and utterly lacking in amenity. Thus the woman who could ride even passably was fortunate in being spared some of the major inconveniences of travel, when travel she must.

When Pisanio reckons Imogen's capabilities at twenty miles a day he is estimating an easy pace, but he is in fact assuming about two-thirds of a normal day's mileage for people who were not travelling at that desperate speed that Spaniards called *matacaballos*. There were as yet no public coaches in England, but in countries where such existed, their daily stages (there was no night travel, if only for reasons of security) were the same as for horsemen and horsewomen. Thus in France, where the first public coach ran from Paris to Orleans in 1571, the journey of about 75 miles took three days.

For the great majority of English people, journeys of such length just did not happen more than a few times in a lifetime. But for both sexes and almost all classes of the rural population (which greatly outnumbered the urban) the commonest journey of all was the weekly excursion to the nearest market. There was then no such thing as a gig; neither had the carrier's cart, which in an age that some people still living today can remember carried village people to the market town once a week, yet made its debut on English roads. There were only two choices – walk or ride – and not only yeomen's wives but the wives of 'husbandmen' (whom we should call small farmers) could either ride pillion behind their husbands or sons or even the farm foremen, or have a horse to themselves. Well, not quite to themselves; if they had any considerable amount of produce to sell there would not be room on it for panniers of butter and eggs or crates of chickens besides two passengers. There would have to be a packhorse as well, and it cannot have been agreeable for the husband to ride the horse with the goodwife clasping him round

'The right butter-women's rank to market.' (The British Library, EG. 1269)

the waist and chattering in his ear while at the same time he was leading another laden horse. Returning, after suitable refreshment following the close of business – 'market-merry' as they say – it must have been next to impossible, what with the wife's shopping as well. Therefore the wives and daughters of husbandmen were encouraged to master the art of equitation at least so far as to be trustable at the helm of a sedate Dobbin, enthroned between two panniers. This is the background of a passage in *As You Like It* which has been variously glossed:

> *Touchstone*:   It is the right butter-women's rank to market.   (III, ii, 95)

Rank makes no sort of sense in a civilian context. In terms of riding it makes one think rather of the line in Michael Drayton's *Polyolbion* (1613–22) about the 'rank-riding Scots upon their galloways', loaded with loot. A suggested reading 'rate' meaning speed or rhythm is better; but unsatisfactory because without precedent elsewhere. The amendment that fits best is 'rack', partly because it is most appropriate to the immediate context. Touchstone is criticising the verses which Rosalind has been reading aloud, with their unrelenting 'rum-ti-tum', not so much in the meter of a trotting horse, the sound of whose hoofs is at least divisible

Pillion riding. Woodcut from Fugger, *Von der Gestüterey*, 1584. (Reproduced by permission of Miland Publishers, Nieuwkoop, Netherlands)

into two-syllable 'feet' as alternate pairs of diagonals hit the ground, but agreeable to the prosody of the rack, the sound of which is heard no more in England, though still in parts of the United States. This is the gait in which each foot hits the road separately, right round the horse from near fore to off-fore: four beats of equal emphasis with an unvarying interval between – one, two, three, four, one, two, three, four. Moreover the rack was suitable for the purpose. It conveyed one at the speed of a trot without the jolting action of the latter or the camel-like swaying of the pace; and a woman who was either using the primitive, non-adhesive side-saddle of the day or was seated astride above two panniers which prevented her using stirrups could travel at the rack in comfort and without smashing the eggs which most 'butter-women' also stocked. So smooth, at best, is this gait that in Puerto Rico, where it is still practised, the deciding test in show contests for 'paso fino' rackers is for the rider to place a full glass of wine on the flat top of his hard hat and make a circuit of the ring without spilling a drop. One should add in fairness that Touchstone's critical comment after the second bout of poesy – 'the very false gallop of verses' (III, ii, 111) – is less apposite. False gallop at this time meant canter. And the lines in question do not at all fit the marked 'tiddly-pom, tiddly-pom' of the canter.

The commonest combination in pillion-riding must have been husband and wife; this is the point of the not very clever cross-talk between Curtis and Grumio in *The Taming of the Shrew*:

> *Grumio*: ... my master riding behind my mistress—
> *Curtis*: Both of one horse? (IV, i, 60)

Of course if they *had* been on one horse he would have been in front. Likewise in *Much Ado*, Dogberry says:

> ... an two men ride of a horse, one must ride behind. (III, v, 35)

The slightly archaic phrasing suggests that this was a proverbial saw. Perhaps the most significant reference to two men on one horse is in *As You Like It*:

> ... both in a tune like two gipsies on a horse. (V, iii, 12)

Not only is this the only passage relating to gypsies in the whole works (in other instances it means Egyptians, and ancient Egyptians at that) but it shows that at this time the Romanies who were later to become the keenest horse-dealers in this island were so poorly provided with *gryes* that they had to ride double when travelling; that is, most of the time.

The belief, not always justified, of travellers that there was safety in numbers is well brought out in this passage:

> ... we'll call up the gentlemen, they will along with company, for they have great charge. (*I Henry IV*, II, i, 43)

MIGRANTS

The Elizabethan and Jacobean governments were implacably hostile to persons of no fixed abode, and such travellers took good care to keep out of the public eye, whatever their means or lack of them. It might be thought that those who were rich enough to be legally possessed of a horse would also be rich enough to come to terms with the law, in the person of the parish constable, wherever encountered. I am not certain that this was the case. Though there were then no Irish tinkers on the English roads, since their advent was one consequence of a war of conquest not accomplished at that time, there were a great many travellers who, though not exactly criminal, had a somewhat equivocal status. People seeking, or dodging, work, who travelled the roads all over England, must have included many from the western and northern periphery of England and from Wales. In these regions horses, or rather ponies, were very cheap and to be had for less than 10s; they had never been corn-fed in their lives and would do very well on roadside grazing. There were also hawkers who were small-time crooks on the side, of which Autolycus (*The Winter's Tale*) is the type. He peddled on foot, but pedlars with their packs on a pony were fairly common. But Travelling People, with capital letters, either Romanies or halfbred diddicoys, were rarely encountered and their number still few. After all the Romany people had been in Britain for less than a century. Besides, at this time they were notoriously short of horses and never had carts. Their typical conveyance then was the ass, and it is possible that the spread of the donkey through England and Wales (the animal was unknown in the West Country until after 1600) was due to gypsy migration.

5

The carriers

It is inappropriate to say that the wheels of English commerce could not have turned, in the last complete decade of Elizabeth I's reign and the first of her successor's, without the carrier, because with few exceptions he did without wheels. The word 'carriage' meant, in substance, his calling; moving goods and merchandise from one place to another on pack-saddles. It is equally true that though carrying was a well-recognised calling, its edges were blurred all round. There were always a great many part-time carriers who were obliged to keep packhorses as part of their business, especially in the cloth-weaving and allied trades, but did not always have full loads and made them up with goods carried for other people. If a husbandman was put out of his arable holding, or lost his horned cattle or sheep by some visitation such as the murrain, he could always pick up some sort of a living with his horses in the carrying trade.

The legal status of carriers was equivocal. A statute of 1571 required licences to be taken out by carriers, but only by such as habitually conveyed certain food-stuffs. This was really only part of the Elizabethan apparatus of price control, which never worked in practice because it flew in the face of economic realities.

Nobody writing on this subject, however briefly, can withhold a debt of acknowledgement to John Crofts, whose *Packhorse, Waggon and Post* (1967) so admirably summarises all that is known of this important subject, especially the complicated legal aspect. To put it briefly, the legally defined calling of 'common carrier' did not exist at this time in the sense that anyone was licensed to carry on that trade. If a carrier wished to escape legal liability for damage or loss of goods entrusted to him, by whatever cause – fire at an inn by night, robbery by the wayside, flood or tempest or snowstorm – he had to make a special arrangement

43

with every separate customer. Common carriers declaring themselves to be such did exist, but only in a few cases where, to quote Crofts, 'they could afford the title only because they enjoyed a virtual monopoly of carriage from a certain town, over a certain route'. The university carriers of Cambridge and Oxford are an example, but their case was very special.

Certainly, a carriers' organisation existed, but it was something of an underground network. Carriers were not a corporation as other trades in cities were, and though their links with the innkeeping trade were close, they did not enjoy the protection of such well-defined liabilities as the innkeepers did. Crofts thinks that the chaotic irregularity of the trade was such that the service they provided could have been ten times as effective as it was, considering the number of horses and amount of gear owned severally by these contractors.

But perhaps this was the inevitable consequence of the sort of men who gravitated to this trade. They were, in a sense, responsible men. But they were also independent by nature, hence not good combiners. They were men who could not easily be intimidated: since the greatest risk was from robbers, and since most robbers relied primarily on frightening their victims by a show of force and were not necessarily prepared to fight it out with them, a man who excelled at saying boo to a goose had the makings of a carrier in him. Other requirements were manifold. Above all he must be a waterproof man. There was no conceivable way in which he could earn a living in carriage without taking a great deal of hard weather right in the face. He must be a good judge of a certain sort of horse, and know where and when to buy it. He must be an expert packer, what was then called a 'ladesman' and in the American West following Mexican custom was known as a 'cargador', able to stow the most varied loads on the packsaddle so that they would neither be smashed *en route* nor spilt by the saddle's shifting over because of unevenly distributed weight. If the knife went on the nearside, the fork must go on the offside. He must be on good, but not intimate, terms with all innkeepers along his route, yet not addicted to the bottle; and he must be ever on the watch against dishonest ostlers who might stint his horses of their provender, or even feed them inferior hay or bread. Above all, he must simply know the way. In an age when road-lighting and signposts did not exist, when a main road was a set of ruts among other sets of ruts of purely agricultural significance, this was of prime importance; and simple familiarity by travelling the same road both ways in all conditions of weather and light, once acquired, was half the battle in successfully establishing oneself in the business.

For reasons of security, all but the strong, the valiant and well-armed preferred to travel in company, and, if there were no private party, to go along with the carriers. Besides, the carriers knew the way everywhere, by day or night, and signposts were few and far between.

Those who were too poor to hire a horse to themselves might occasionally secure half its use, either going 'ride and tie' with a companion or riding one behind the other. Or again they might have recourse to the carriers, sitting above the load in excruciating discomfort, the legs horizontal on top of the pannier either side. This mode of travel was still in use in the eighteenth century.

⧫ ⧫ ⧫

'Touch a galled horse on the back, and he will kick' was one of the old sayings collected by William Camden in his *Remains*, and there are many echoes of it in the works of Shakespeare. There are also some hints as to how the horse might come by his galls.

> I prithee, Tom, beat Cut's saddle, put a few flocks in the point; poor jade is wrung in the withers out of all cess. (*I Henry IV* II, i, 5)

Cut is a packhorse, and evidently by his name a gelding. The pack-saddle consisted of a primitive 'tree', two inverted wooden forks joined by bars, under which was a flock-stuffed pad (the better sort of saddles were stuffed with hair). The point was the fore-end of this pad. When the stuffing shifted the front fork pinched ('wrung') the withers. The pad was beaten to redistribute the stuffing.

> Let the galled jade wince, our withers are unwrung (III, ii, 237)

said Hamlet, making verbal play with this very situation.

The dialogue from *I Henry IV* referred to above takes place in the inn-yard at Rochester, probably about the middle of May, and at four o'clock in the morning there is still an hour to go before sunrise. Yet the master-carrier is dismayed that his 'horse' (the old plural) are not yet loaded. The train ought to be on the road at sunrise, if he is to 'go to bed with a candle' (II, i, 42) in London. Sunset at nine o'clock, allowing two hours at the destination for unloading, for feeding, watering and bedding-down the horses, for the carriers' supper and a drink or two by the fireside: this gives one the same fourteen-hour travelling day, including two halts for refreshment and 'baiting' the horses, as had been customary for Chaucer's pilgrims travelling the same road two hundred years earlier. Travelling meant a long day which when shortened perforce in winter simply meant more days on the road.

There are the eternal complaints about the quality of lodgings and in particular about the horse-feed supplied by the inn – 'Peas and beans are as dank here as a dog' – and lament that things are not what they used to be, at least since 'Robin Ostler died. Poor fellow never joyed since the price of oats rose' (II, i, 8–11). The twenty-eight miles or so between Rochester and London are still being covered at the rate of about two miles in the hour, because the fuel supplied by Robin's successors in office is not exactly high octane. But the truth is, it never was. The proportion of peas and beans, even when not dog-dank, was always too high relative to the amount of oats, even when the latter were at their cheapest.

This scene in *I Henry IV* tells us a great deal about the life of the carriers and especially the more dreary aspects of it. Carriers were the backbone of English commercial life, and in Elizabethan times were operating under almost the same conditions as had obtained in the days of Richard II, when a great deal of legislation had been enacted concerning such matters as the hiring of horses, responsibilities of innkeepers and similar affairs of the first importance to carriers, most of which was still in force. Carriers were still for the most part working without vehicles of any kind, in and out of London, to fixed timetables, a complete schedule of which (expressed in terms of days rather than of hours) may be found in the works of John Taylor, the seventeenth-century 'water poet'. According to John Stow, regular carrier services using 'long wagons' had come into use by 1584 but only on the Canterbury road, no doubt 'lying' at Rochester as did these carriers in *I Henry IV*; but they still handled only a small part of the trade. In 1597, when *I Henry IV* was probably written, the current law as it affected carriers had been formulated not later than the actual reign of that monarch, and it simply did not envisage long hauls by wagon. Official regulations in this matter did not catch up with the changing situation until the 1630s and, in the lifetime of Shakespeare, carriers like most English horsemen were still living and working within a late medieval framework which was coming loose at the joints.

6

Harness and draught

Carts

Intolerable noise was inseparable from the cart most of the time. The more modern type of axle was fixed to the cart body and terminated in iron or iron-shod stubs, on which the hubs of the wheels revolved individually. In this type the hub was lubricated from a horn containing horse-fat, or in some districts tar. In the older style of cart, perhaps already in Shakespeare's time restricted to the more backward hill regions of the West and North, the wheels had no spokes but were of almost solid planking and were fixed to each end of the axle-tree by wedges. The axle-tree itself revolved in between pegs on the under-side of the cart, and the noise made by this was so characteristic that it was never forgotten, once heard. Thus in the memoirs of the geologist Adam Sedgwick, written in his old age about his childhood in the Dent Valley of Yorkshire (now Cumbria) about 1800, we find:

> The axle-trees ... revolved between the pegs as the cart dragged on, with a horrible amount of friction that produced a creaking noise, in the expressive language of the Dales called 'jyking'. The friction was partly relieved by frequent doses of tar administered to the pegs from a ram's horn. Horrible were the creakings and jykings which set all teeth on edge.

The distribution of the little 'tumble-cars' with their 'clog' wheels was very restricted by 1800, but in 1600 they were the only form of agricultural transport in the region of the Welsh border beyond the Severn and only fifty miles west of Stratford, and in the greater part of the North of England; also in the southwestern peninsula, about as far as the longitude of Start Point in Devon. Between there and Land's End there were only sleds, and no wheels at all.

An example of the more modern type of cart with fixed axle and spoke wheels

Two-wheeled cart in the streets of London, watercolour by Michael Van Meer. (Edinburgh University Library)

revolving on the axle-arms is seen in our illustration by Van Meer, a water-colour done by him in the streets of London, probably three years after Shakespeare left the town for ever. That need not worry us on grounds of anachronism. But for the curious fore-structure built up on the shafts over the rump of the horse, neither cart nor harness differs in any material respect from that shown in the miniatures of the Luttrell Psalter, painted in 1340 or earlier. The wheels have ten spokes and hubs with the lynch-pins clearly visible. The rim is a composite one, consisting of ten short felloes or segments. Distributed as shown, the load is practically being carried by the horse, since all the weight is in front of the axle. Carts of this design were to be found working in the Scottish Highlands until well into the nineteenth century. Drays were also to be seen on the London streets, but the dray of those times, though used by brewers among other trades, was not a cart but a sled, big enough to carry one hogshead and drawn by one horse. The advantage of this sled in the carriage of heavy loads was its low loading platform. Whatever municipal scavenging went on was also performed by drays.

The swimming of a witch, showing a long-bodied cart – or the wreck of it – used as a substitute for a wagon in some parts of the country. Woodcut from *Witches Apprehended, Examined*, an anonymous seventeenth-century pamphlet.

Wagons

Other types of cart and wagons were in use in various parts of the country. The hybrid long cart, called in Somerset until recently a 'cartwain', had the long body of a wagon on the single axle of a cart. The one shown in our illustration of a witch being ducked has, in the lines of the bodywork, the characteristic profile of the English box-wagon which was quite different from the crate-like cart-body and equally different from the trough-shaped body of continental wagon-types. Four-wheeled harvest wagons were in use in those counties, mostly southeastern, where the ground was flat and where cereal crops were of more importance than livestock. Some already had the high hind-wheels and low fore-wheels, permitting a narrower turning circle, that was characteristic of the English farm-wagon at the most sophisticated nineteenth-century stage of its evolution. But most had four wheels all the same size, with all the technical drawbacks inherent therein.

This feature was shared by the chariotte, a vehicle which became obsolete in the lifetime of William Shakespeare, and was superseded by the coche or caroche. But at the Queen's accession it had been still the only kind of road-going vehicle available even to the highest in the land, and was used also for solemn processions. Its design had not been altered by so much as a nail since the days of Richard II or earlier, and it was almost identical with the 'pagaunt-wains' on which scenes from the earliest English dramas, the miracle plays, had been enacted at street-corners in York, Chester and Coventry. In so far as they continued to be used after the introduction of the coach it was in this sort of role – as 'floats' carrying allegorical costumed figures in pageants – and also as hearses. They were drawn by four or five or six Great Horses in single file, a formation difficult to manage even at a

'The vi horses drawing the firste chariott' for the accession of Elizabeth I – not occupied because the ladies it was intended for preferred to ride sidesaddle. (College of Arms, MS.M.6, fo. 40v)

Scarce contemporary reproductions of a coach driven from the box (left) and another type driven by a postillion (right). Detail from Hoefnagel, *Nonsuch Palace*. (Reproduced by courtesy of the Trustees of the British Museum)

walk, the ultimate in tandems. The driver himself usually rode the wheel-horse, and his mate the one behind the fore-horse. Neither of them held the reins of any horse but the one they were riding; all the unridden horses had ordinary riding-reins, looped over the peak of the horse-collar. Traction by all except the wheeler was by a single pair of traces (wainropes) about 50 ft long. Such a team could only be managed safely at a walk, and with difficulty at a trot. What happened in town work, for instance, when the first two horses had gone around a sharp corner?

Coaches, caroches
The coach shows technological features which had long been commonplace in Danubian lands, combined with special characteristics of a Hungarian village called Kocs, famous for its skilled wheelwrights, and the design of its harvest wagons. The driver did not ride any of the horses but sat in the vehicle. He had the reins of the whole team in his hand all the time. There were no shafts but a central

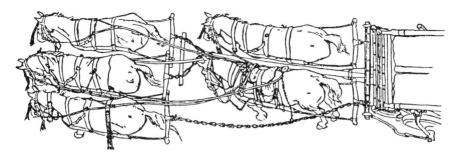

Sketch by A. Garay showing Central European method of yoking a five-in-hand. This method of harnessing a team for four-wheeled vehicles was used exclusively for the coach in its country of origin, but does not appear to have been adopted in England at the same time as the coach, being introduced very much later. (Reproduced by permission of Harrap Limited)

Londoners fleeing the plague in a coach with small, fully locking fore-wheels. Contemporary woodcut.

draft-pole for the pair of wheelers, before which the other pairs could be harnessed by means of swingle-trees, which were also used to include spare single horses in the team, as in the sketch by A. Garay which shows the Central European method of yoking a five-in-hand. This habit of using five- or seven-in-hand teams was not adopted along with the rest of the Magyar technique: Westerners stuck to even numbers. Of course draft-pole and swingle-(whipple-)trees as such were familiar enough in England. It was their combination in the context of passenger transport that was so novel and effective, as were the small, fully locking fore-wheels.

There were no English-built coaches in the reign of Elizabeth I or of James I. The best were Hungarian or Bohemian (Dr John Dee, the mathematician and astrologer who served as official soothsayer to Mary I and Elizabeth I, brought one back from his travels in Silesia and Poland) but the majority were German-made imitations, largely from Mecklenburg. They were nothing near so light as the

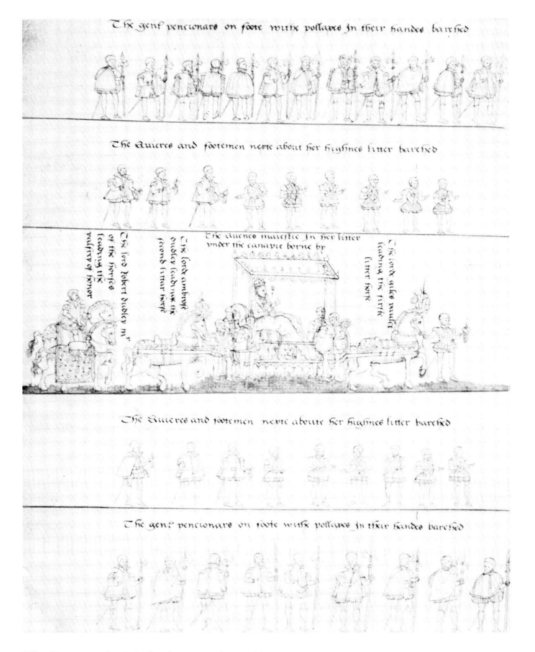

'The Quenes maiestie in her litter' as planned for the accession of Elizabeth I. This, no more than the 'chariott', was in fact used, as the Queen also preferred to ride. (College of Arms, MS.M.6, fo. 41v)

original *kocsi*. No coaches had glass windows. None had springs at this time, but hung in leather slings.

By the end of Elizabeth I's reign, all great houses had coaches, but few owners got value for their money. For example, the Cecils had at least three in 1610: the riche caroche, which was gilded, the olde caroche, and Lady Cranborne's caroche. All formed part of the town establishment, but few of the old town palaces along the Strand had room for a coach-house, or even room for a coach to manoeuvre in the yard. Thus 'garaging' had to be found away from the town house, and there are frequent references in account books of the period to rent paid for coach-houses and coach-horse stabling in the vicinity of St Martin's Lane. It was only in the 1970s that the sign 'Aldridge's Horse Repository' was taken down from a building, since demolished, in the upper part of the Lane. Aldridge's was an auction mart still specialising in coach-horses early in the present century; together with Parker's harness-making establishment just across the street (still in business), it was the last survivor of a great complex of coach-building and harness-making and ancillary trades once concentrated in the Long Acre/St Martin's Lane quarter, hard by the old Royal Mews which stood on the site of the present National Gallery. This part of London, on the edge of Leicester Fields, was simply the nearest point to the court at Whitehall and to most of the great town houses in the Strand that afforded room for the carriages of the nobility at the end of the sixteenth century.

Mention in the Cecil papers of the coach being used further away from London than Theobalds or Hatfield is rare. It occurs only once in Robert Cecil's lifetime when there is a note of a journey to Bath, but there are more frequent mentions of his having gone to take the waters there in his horse-litter, and this is the conveyance more frequently found in executors' inventories of great estates further away from the capital than Surrey. For instance, the inquisition post mortem of the 9th Earl of Northumberland's chattels at Petworth in Sussex, taken as late as 1632, included among livestock working horses and thirty brood mares with fifteen foals. The inventory of the buildings includes a 'coache house'; but its contents were listed only as a two-horse litter, with its gear. The coaches bequeathed in the Earl's will were all in London.

The horses which drew the coach were in most instances Great Horses of the kind that otherwise would be used under saddle for military purposes, or in peacetime for ceremonial purposes 'of state'. These by tradition were all stallions, but there were inherent difficulties about driving four or six entire males in close proximity to each other: to meet on the road a mare in season would have been the coachman's nightmare. The adoption of coaching did much to break down the prejudice, inherent in England, against the use of geldings by gentlemen, and with the adoption of the Hungarian coach team went the Hungarian practice of castration, hitherto only customary in England for animals of more humble status.

But the coach was restricted not so much by the limitations of its design or harness or by the quality of the horses in the team. It simply could not make headway along English roads with their combination of bullock-worn ruts, pot-holes and quagmires, the product of the frequent rainfall and of a system of maintenance whereby no authority above parish level was responsible for upkeep; and of all parish offices that of waywarden was the most reluctantly undertaken and perfunctorily performed. Nobody wanted a job which entailed impressing his neighbours' transport and labour force.

Steep gradients were daunting. A nobleman travelling in his coach could hardly ever be able to get up a hill of any length without recourse to extra 'yokes', either of horses or cattle, lent by local husbandmen. Unless these happened to be tenants of his lordship, such hire could come expensive.

Water obstacles also played their part. In general, routes chosen would have to go from ford to ford, because the ordinary one-arched, steeply peaked packhorse bridge, specially of the North Country, was impassable to coaches. Even in London where, as in most other towns, the standard of paving was high enough to make reasonable going for the coach, the only bridge over the Thames had not been built to take coaches. If my Lord wished to take his coach to the theatre from his lodging somewhere in the Strand, it was easy enough to get to any of the theatres in the Fields, out on the Middlesex side, but the Bankside theatres only just across the water could only be reached by taking the ferry, which landed at Lambeth and driving all the way east to Southwark. Coaches did not save time, and they swallowed money (it cost 8s to shoe a coach team in 1610 and a new set of shoes lasted only a month), but as a status symbol they were unequalled. Responsible statesmen, judges, preachers, might fulminate against the coach making adultery easier, using up horses of a stamp that ought to have been available to the State, being 'able and sufficient for service in the warres', and impeding the martial ability of young gentlemen. But those who could afford to use them, and be seen using them, would not be deterred from coach travel. 'Yet there has been knights, and lords, and gentlemen', said Mistress Quickly, 'with their coaches – I warrant you, coach after coach' (*Merry Wives of Windsor* II, ii, 60). Before 1560 there had not been a single coach in England, yet by the turn of the century, not only every innkeeper in the country but every other tradesman was as ready as his Victorian counterpart to classify customers according to whether or not they were 'carriage folk'.

Let it be borne in mind that there was no alternative to the coach, other than riding or the litter, at any season of the year. On the Continent, and especially east

Cart with fore-horse and fill-horse, an archaic pattern only surviving in the far north and west.

of the Rhine, once winter had properly set in, faster speeds and smoother going could be achieved by a sleigh, as also in parts of Scandinavia, and even in the Low Countries where the skating season was also the season for the racing of sleighs drawn by fast-trotting light horses on the ice of rivers, lakes and canals. But the expedient of the sledded Polacks was not available to the English with their mild and sodden climate, at least not often enough to be relied on. And there was no such thing, at any season of the year, as a fast, light, smart, one-horse carriage. For one thing, there were no springs. 'Gig' in the language of the time meant only a whirly-gig, that is a whipping-top; and it was to be more than a hundred years before the hubs of any English conveyance revolved fast enough to spin around like tops and thus cause light passenger carts to be called gigs.

       📖 📖 📖

> Either I am
> The fore-horse in the team, or I am none
> That draw i'th' sequent trace. (*Two Noble Kinsmen* I, ii, 58–60)

These lines probably belong to the Shakespearian part of *The Two Noble Kinsmen*, not only because of the general flavour of the language, but because they contain another example of Shakespeare's metaphorical fore-horses: by this time, at the very end of his writing career, he was tending to repeat himself in the matter of imagery. In *All's Well That Ends Well*, written some dozen years earlier, he had made Bertram say:

> I shall stay here the forehorse to a smock. (II, i, 30)

'If I become not a cart as well as another man...' – an English hanging during the reign of Henry VIII.

The fore-horse is the team-mate of Old Gobbo's 'fill-horse' (*Merchant of Venice* II, ii, 91) mentioned in Chapter 3 above, and as we saw there the term implies the harnessing of two horses in line ahead, or in tandem, with shafts. This is one of the only two instances where Shakespeare uses the word 'trace'; otherwise he calls the same item a wainrope, which is its Anglo-Saxon name (*waegnrap*). Traces might be either of chain or leather or rope, and those harness parts which had been called in Anglo-Saxon *rapas* were either leather or vegetable fibre, but they were round in section, not flat straps.

How closely Shakespearian figures of speech stick to the realities of agricultural and equestrian life, the more so when the images are traditional and not original, is shown in this very context of traces. In Chapter 1 we pointed to the blurred unrealistic metaphor of the post-mechanical age, 'Wild horses will not drag it from me'. Sir Toby Belch was no intellectual giant, nor greatly acquainted with physical effort of any kind except elbow-lifting; yet even he knows better than that, when he says:

> I think oxen and wainropes cannot hale them together.
>
> (*Twelfth Night* III, ii, 57)

All carters knew that although horses might go faster and further in a day, under certain circumstances, especially deep mud, oxen had greater pulling power than horses of the same weight. Launce in *Two Gentlemen of Verona* says:

> a team of horse shall not pluck that from me.   (III, i, 264)

It makes a change, but he is really putting his money on the outsiders.

The most sinister employment of carts, that which the hangman made of them, is mentioned by Falstaff in *I Henry IV*:

> If I become not a cart as well as another man, a plague on my bringing up! I hope I
> shall as soon be strangled with a halter as another.   (II, iv, 490)

The excruciating noise of the ungreased cart in motion is also mentioned in the same play, where Hotspur makes his philistine declaration of faith against all music, singing and 'mincing poetry'. Rather than hear his fellow-rebel Glendower sing 'an English ditty lovely well' to the harp, he would hear 'a dry wheel grate on the axle-tree' (III, i, 119, 126). A very un-Northumbrian avowal, coming from the county of the bagpipes; but otherwise quite appropriate, since Northumberland then produced some of the best horses in England but had the most primitive carts. These were the ones where the axle itself tumbled and shrieked under the cart, in one piece with the wheels. However, this kind cannot be meant here, because it is the wheel (or rather its nave) that grates against the axle-tree at its junction with the axle-arm: so the axle is not turning with the wheels, as in carts of the utmost rusticity.

There is some slight indication that the wagon itself was not a familiar sight to Shakespeare. He never used the word, or the word 'wagoner', except by way of metaphor, and then usually in unsuitable contexts, mostly classical. This is due in some measure to the ignorance then prevailing, even among scholars, of the nature of transport in the ancient world. Titus Andronicus says 'And then I'll come and be thy waggoner' (*Titus Andronicus* V, ii, 48) because the playwright, like many scholars who published translations of the classics (for instance, Sir Thomas North as Philemon Holland), thought of the antique chariot as something with four wheels (in *Hamlet*, the sun's mythological chariot is called a 'cart', which is two wheels nearer the mark). The confusion probably arose from the filtering of Latin expressions through French, in which language *chariot* means a farm wagon with four wheels, and was the origin of the English chariotte such as we mentioned above as the processional vehicle of pre-Elizabethan days. For what it is worth, there is no traditional type of wagon known in Warwickshire, and the classic *English Farm Wagon* by J. Geraint Jenkins lists three different types in use in that county after Shakespeare's time, all named after other shires. The wagon was thus an unfamiliar sight to the young Shakespeare because it only penetrated Warwickshire from adjacent counties as a part of agricultural improvements a century and more after his death.

So we come to the coach, which must have been familiar enough to Shakespeare in his London days. Except in two passages, it is only mentioned in connection with the most delicate phantasies. In *Love's Labour's Lost*, the King says:

> Thou shin'st in every tear that I do weep:
> No drop but as a coach doth carry thee.   (IV, iii, 32)

The confusion of coach, chariot and wagon is seen at its height in the oft-quoted speech of Mercutio about Mab, Queen of the Fairies:

> Her *chariot* is an empty hazelnut
> Made by the joiner squirrel or old grub,
> Time out o' mind the fairies' *coachmakers*;
> Her *waggon*-spokes made of long spinners' legs,
> The cover of the wings of grasshoppers,
> Her traces of the smallest spider web,
> Her collars of the moonshine's watery beams,
> Her whip of cricket's bone, the lash of film,
> Her *waggoner*, a small grey-coated gnat.   (*Romeo & Juliet* I, v, 59–67)

To be fair, I do not know any author who at this date (early 1590s) uses the word coachman, or recall any instance of its use before 1630; only Yeoman of the Coche, a kind of foreman of the department, much too grand to drive himself. It seems as if wagoner meant the driver of any four-wheeled vehicle (replacing the earlier 'chariotte-man') and carter the driver of a two-wheeled turn-out.

Woodcut illustrating the coachman on the box, the really superior feature of the Hungarian invention.

The only proprietors of real-life coaches in the entire works are at first sight unlikely to be such. The first is Ophelia, in dark-age Denmark, and she, poor dear, only calls for hers when she is as mad as a hatter. The second is Portia, the richest as well as the cleverest of Shakespeare's heroines. It is worth mentioning what the capabilities of these coaches were expected to be.

> When I am in my coach, which stays for us
> At the park gate; and therefore haste away,
> For we must measure twenty miles today.
>
> (*Merchant of Venice* III, iv, 82)

Twenty miles from Belmont to the ferry terminus for Venice: this matches fairly well with the letter sent from Lord Salisbury to his son in 1608, coming down from Cambridge: 'If you will have coaches sent for you on Fryday night at Stansted [Essex] then you may be in London on Saturday night': again, about twenty miles. But in order to get a good start on Saturday morning, the coach must be ready the night before. Coach travel was unsuitable for matters of life and death. The coach was not the instrument for able-bodied men to execute the business of state with due dispatch.

Can it be that Shakespeare was of the reactionary but widely held opinion that the coach was not a fit conveyance for heroes, and so assigns them only to his heroines? Similarly, litters are for the old and the sick, and as such they are used by Lear and King John as well as Uther Pendragon (in *I Henry VI* III, ii, 95).

Neither Shakespeare nor any contemporary used 'carriage', except 'gun-carriage', in the context of transport, otherwise than as an abstract noun meaning conveyance, usually by packhorse. Nor does he mention drays, but draymen occur in *Troilus and Cressida* and *Richard II*, in both cases in a rather pejorative sense, and probably scavengers are meant.

7

Magnificence and the equine ideal

PERFORMANCE AND CONFORMATION

'Many horses are requisite for a king', Hugh Latimer had said, preaching before the Queen's brother Edward. By that he had not meant the thousands of animals of all types that were necessary to carry on the business of the realm in peace and in war, but the inner circle of horses such as had appeared in medieval account rolls as *equi intrinseci*, which transported the royal household and the person of the sovereign. Shakespeare's Queen and her brother and sister had had the most rigorous and comprehensive education that the age of Henry VIII could devise, with a curriculum for teenagers that would greatly overtax the modern undergraduate. Their father was so gifted and so omnicompetent himself that he could chop logic with scholars and play the lute against minstrels on equal terms – at least in his own estimation – and he was determined that his children too should be polymaths. Four modern and two antique languages was the minimum requirement. Yet time had to be found in their overcrowded learning day for frequent and intensive riding lessons.

English equitation in that century and the following one was of two kinds. The first, 'snaffle-riding', was for utility and for fun. It had to be learnt, but most upper-class children learnt it almost unconsciously, through the pores of the skin, for it was practised on the palfrey or 'ambling pad' which did not trot but paced, thus giving a very smooth ride, with a rather rocking motion. Even the palfreys ridden by adults were only ponies, by our standards, rarely more than fourteen hands high, and they came in all sizes below that. There was nothing particularly royal or even aristocratic about that sort of riding. This was the way gentlemen

Palfrey with sidesaddle, racking at speed. Woodcut from Fugger, *Von der Gestüterey*, 1584.
(Reproduced by permission of Miland Publishers, Nieuwkoop, Netherlands)

and yeomen, husbandmen and urban tradesmen rode about their everyday business. Everyone rode that way when hunting or hawking. You just sat there, whatever speed the horse moved at. Or so it seemed, though of course there was more to it than that.

This was the oldest style of riding and it went back in direct line to the practice of the antique world. It was a style (with, behind it, a manner of breaking horses to the saddle) devised in a world which knew of no such thing as a stirrup, and therefore avoided trotting at all costs. It went back at least to the middle of the Iron Age, when the Britons first took the ponies out from under the chariot yoke and rode them with hardly such a thing as a saddle between back and buttock.

But the children of the nobility had to learn another style of riding that was indeed 'requisite for a king', as soon as reasonably possible. They had to learn how

James I in procession going to open Parliament, on what appears to be a courser of state not betraying much evidence of Spanish, Neapolitan or Oriental blood. Watercolour by Michael Van Meer. (Edinburgh University Library)

to sit on what Sir Thomas Elyot called 'great and rough horses', rough in this sense meaning trotting instead of pacing. Down to some time in the reign of Henry VII no one would ride a Great Horse, the mount of the knight in his military capacity, unless he were actually at war, training for it, or imitating it in a tourney; but slowly during the sixteenth century the fashion grew of riding the Great Horse on occasions of peaceful ceremony or 'state'. To do this one required stirrups (and to use the stirrups) and not a snaffle but a curb bit, then of such severity that it had to be used with finesse and discretion. For this reason alone the boy or girl could not graduate to this school of equitation before reaching the age of at any rate a certain discretion. Furthermore, there was no such thing as a miniature Great Horse (Velázquez painted one, the Infante Don Balthasar up, but it is a creature of his fancy). No doubt the style would be learned on a quiet old Great Horse, but even so the pupil must have legs long enough for his heels to impinge on more or less the

Painted a score of years after Shakespeare's death, this is a brilliantly imaginative representation of the miniature Great Horse in which I do not believe. *Velàzquez, Prince Balthasar Carlos*, 1635. (Prado Museum, Madrid)

The henchmen

A lively representation of 'riding gentlemen' in the royal service executing high school airs, including the capriole and the levade. The henchmen at the accession of Queen Elizabeth I. (College of Arms, MS.M.6, fo. 35v)

right area of the horse's sides. No one rose to the trot, but 'sat it out', and this alone dictated a different seat from that of the 'snaffle-riding' horseman.

Even so, the manner of riding the Great Horse was not simply that of the knights of old. The technique had been elaborated and modified since the Renaissance by Italian, Spanish and French riding-masters, to include all manner of airs and graces known in the English of Shakespeare's contemporaries collectively as 'gambading'. The purpose of gambading was, quite frankly, showing off. It was to display the royal or noble person to the best advantage, to give the impression that he was controlling with consummate art and sang-froid a steed with whose mettle no ordinary mortal could cope. The 'henchmen' or professional nagsmen are seen doing this in the Heralds' Manuscript (illustrated) which shows the royal household in procession at the Queen's accession. They are displaying 'airs above the ground' in the modern parlance of the High School – but then called 'bounds' – including such elegancies as the levade, the croupade, even the capriole, in all of which the horse rears up in front or kicks out behind so as not to be supported on more than two legs. Sovereigns less robust in body or spirit than the Tudors might not attempt this, but keep the feet of their 'courser of state' in a normal relationship to the ground. However, noblemen who wished to shine in the royal presence outdoors must be masters of the whole repertoire of 'gambading'. Consequently not only must they be trained in youth but they must maintain in the household henchmen, sometimes called 'riding gentlemen' (or 'gentlemen riders', a phrase which has a different meaning in our day), to train their gambading horses in such antics. It was all an essential part of what John Skelton in old King Harry's time had called 'Magnificence'.

Illutris Robertus
Dudleius, comes
Leicestriæ, baro
Denbigh, &c.
obijt anno 1588.

Robert Dudley, Earl of Leicester. Among other offices, he filled that of Master of the Horse to Queen Elizabeth I. Engraving by R. Vaughn. (National Museum of Wales, Cardiff)

From this point of view the coach would never quite do for a Great Man what a good gambading horse did. He might go about town in his coach (indeed he hardly went anywhere else in it) but one was not so obviously *seen* in it as one was on horseback. For this reason the custom of painting the owner's coat of arms on the coach door was fashionable from an early date. There was no glass in the windows, so that in bad weather one either had to face the rain or sit in darkness behind leather curtains, one's countenance unseen by the vulgar. Still, with one's quarterings prominently blazoned on the coach door, one could send the equipage lumbering round the town empty, or carrying only a friend or a gentleman of the household, and the citizens would still say 'There goeth my Lord Bogwater his coach. Cost him seventy pound as I heard tell.'

Nobody really cared what the palfrey looked like so long as it was handy and gave a comfortable ride at all gaits, whether pacing or racking; nor the hunter, so long as it was clever and could go all day at the very moderate speeds which deer-park hunting and hare-hunting in the open country demanded; nor the racehorse, which as a type was just beginning to be differentiated in the last decade of Shakespeare's lifetime. But to the 'Great Man' and his dependants, the conformation, the make and shape of the courser of state were of prime importance. It is for horses of this function that aesthetic standards of the exterior were laid down, and the innumerable descriptions of the ideal type are meant only to apply to such horses. The search for horses of 'stately' appearance and of such quality as would enable them to be trained for all branches of 'gambading' on behalf of persons with pretensions to nobility was constant, the more so as selective breeding by private persons was in its infancy, and the desired type was as likely to be found tucked away somewhere, the result of haphazard mating, as by recourse to a breed of renown such as Lord Willoughby's. How far the specifications laid down in 'literary' sources were of any use for purposes of selection will be discussed later. Suffice to say here that some of the best-known and oftenest quoted were of no practical import whatever.

The traditional points of a good horse, itemised and not all agreed with by Nicholas Morgan, take up ten pages of his *Perfection*, number thirty-three and can be condensed as follows:

> Hoofs black, smooth, dry, large, round and hollow. Coronets small. Pasterns short. Joints big, with long 'fetlocks' (what is now called 'feather'). Legs straight. Knees big. Thighs sinewy. Shoulders long, large and full of flesh. Breast broad. Neck long and tapering towards the head, arched. Ears small, sharp, upright. Forehead broad. Eyes large and black. No hollow above the eye. Jaws slender. Nostrils open, the nasal passages ample. The mouth large. The shape of the head like that of a ram. Mane thin and long. Withers straight and sharp. Back short and level. Sides long and large. Belly long 'orderly hidden under the ribs'. Flanks full. Rump round and level. Thighs large

and long. Hams lean, dry and straight. Tail full, reaching to the ground. The dock (truncheon) well set on. Genitals small. The general proportions 'like a stag', that is, the hindquarters slightly lower than the forehand.

Often such descriptions are at direct variance with the rather sparse evidence of equestrian portraiture. To display the heroic figure to the best advantage the horse must be as tall as possible or credible. Most of the 'classic' descriptions of make and shape lay stress on short pasterns and cannon bones. Yet court artists mostly drew these impossibly long, because the easiest way to draw a 'high horse' is to put it, anatomically speaking, on stilts.

At this time there was no question of a *querelle des anciens et des modernes* in France or England or anywhere else.* It went without saying that everything antique had been superior to its modern equivalent; and yet the educated Englishman had in many ways created a 'superior antique man' in his own image. Among other things, he had a conception of the 'superior antique horseman' (say, Alexander) that was a mirror image of the West European cavalier of post-feudal times. It was obligatory, in writing a book about horsemanship, for instance, to devote a minimum of four or five pages to a name-dropping review of great horsemen of Greek and Roman vintage in Chapter 1, and of their horses, as the object of emulation. It occurred to nobody, in the sixteenth century, that ancient horsemanship had been much more like the 'snaffle-riding' described by only a few provincial masters such as William Browne than Renaissance equitation as practised by Frederigo Grisone and his Neapolitan school. In particular they had no inkling of the difference between antique driving and harness work and that of their own day. This is nowhere more apparent than in Sir Thomas North's Plutarch (1579), in which the translator found nothing inappropriate in applying the word 'coche' to the string of racing chariots kept by the Athenian Alcibiades; as if the single-axle, stripped-to-the-bone hippodrome sulky had anything in common with the lumbering four-wheeled German-made caroches, a race between which, if one ever happened, must have been something like the traction-engine meetings of our own day.

It is difficult to arrive at the total number of horses in the royal establishment at this period since it is often far from clear which of the court functionaries was provided with a horse from the royal stables to carry out his duties, and which were expected to mount themselves. Financially it made little difference to the palace accounts whose property these horses were, so long as they were being found in forage and fodder and bedding, not to speak of attendance, since the

---

* This began in France in the late seventeenth century, when the daring idea was put forward that some modern literature might be as good as that of the ancient Greeks and Romans. It later spread to the whole cultural complex.

'Queen Elizabeth, the defeat of the Spanish Armada', painting of the Tilbury muster, 1588.
(St Faith's Church, Gaywood, King's Lynn)

equation was true then as it is today, namely that it costs as much to keep any riding horse by the year as to buy an ordinary utility animal. Probably Elizabeth's household never at any time had so many horses in its stables as did Henry VIII's at inflationary moments caused by the King's preparations for his grandiose, unnecessary and unprofitable military excursions to France or Flanders. By contrast, it seems the greatest external crisis of Elizabeth's reign necessitated only one extra horse for the Queen to ride on her inspection of the defence forces at Tilbury, and that she borrowed from the Cecils; its portrait (Grey Tilbury) may still be seen at Hatfield House. But in normal times the establishments of the Queen and her father were about of equal size. Both were greatly in excess of that kept by her grandfather.

We have a fair indication of how modest this was in the detailed directions issued, and probably drafted, by Henry VII himself, for the 'Entertainment' of Katherine of Aragon when she came to be married to Arthur, Prince of Wales, in October 1501. To convey the Princess and her retinue from the Tower to the west door of St Paul's the following were ordered:

A Rich Litter for the Princess	4 horses
3 Horsemen in Sidesaddle and Harness	3
A fair Palfrey with a Pillion	1
Eleven Palfreys in one suit for the attending Ladies	11

Grey Tilbury's portrait at Hatfield House; carefully painted in isolation and with the groom
standing in the background, which helps to disguise how small the horse really was.
(Reproduction by courtesy of The Marquess of Salisbury. Photograph: Courtauld Institute of Art)

5 charres diversely apparelled,	
for Ladies and Gentlemen	20 or 30
Betwixt every of the said charres	
five or six Palfreys	20 or 24
	= 59 or 73

Since no picture of the 'charres' used on this occasion, or of any others of that
reign, survives, we do not know whether they had teams of four or of six horses. It

was probably the larger number, since detailed realistic pictures of such vehicles – the English prestige equipage of the pre-coach era – both of Edward II's time and at the accession of Queen Elizabeth, show them as six 'at length', that is, tandem. But even the smaller number was beyond the normal resources of Henry VII's stables, for the directive to the master of ceremonies laid down that 'some wise and expert person be assigned by the King and Queen for the purveyance of the said litter, palfreys, charres and the apparels that shall be necessary for the same, and that this be done with all speed, for the cause it requireth'. Purveyance was a characteristically Tudor financial device whereby the Crown purchased goods from subjects at special cut prices and on long-term credit; but this convenient machinery was no longer in working order in Shakespeare's lifetime except in the limited field of war supplies including remounts, rations and forage for the army.

Though there was no royal coach (perhaps no coach in England at all) at the time of Queen Elizabeth's accession, there was at least one on the establishment for the greater part of her reign, but we know very little about it, except that it was probably six-horsed. The Queen did not really enjoy using it, and probably most of its work was done while it was put at the disposal of those foreign envoys in London whose masters from time to time the Queen desired to think well of her. The real work of royal progresses and state appearances was done by saddle horses. Towards the end of the reign, about the time when *Henry V* and *Much Ado* were written, the Queen was less active and the Court less mobile than it had been twenty years earlier, but it is only for 1598 that we have a detailed inventory of horses in the Windsor stables. The Cecil Papers contain a list, as of October that year, as follows:

A Note of Such Horses as are in the Stables
Gueldings
Grey Poole
Black Wilford — for her Maties Saddle
my la: Marquess
my la: Warwick
my la: Kildare
my la: Stafford
my la: Gylforde
my la: Skydamore
A Bay that my younge La: of Southampton rode
Rone Howard – for M^ris Elizab: Russell
White Howard – for M^ris Anstoe
Grey Fytton – for M^ris Fytton
Bay Compton – for M^ris Ratcliff
White Smythfyeld – for M^ris Carye
Bay Downer – for M^ris Russell
Grey Marcom – for M^ris Hyde

Grey Bellowes
Grey North
Bay Ognoll
Bay Egerton
A Bay of Sir Thomas Garrettes
Bay Osborne

Ij coltes of foure and five yere ould
the stoole horse
A male horse
Bottel horses iij
Dun Howard A double gueldinge to be caste
Grey Frome to be caste   *October 1598*

It consists almost entirely of geldings, since they were now considered the most suitable mounts for ladies, and the prestige of the gelding as such, which had been making slow progress since the reign of Henry VII (before which time geldings in England were rare and of no account), was undoubtedly helped by the long period in which the immediate entourage of the sovereign was largely feminine. There are now only two for the Queen's personal use, because she hardly hunts any more. There are six ridden by peeresses, their own property and not that of the Crown, and fourteen royal geldings, for the use of ladies in waiting of lesser rank, half of them assigned to particular ladies and the rest spare, for disposal as necessary. Two more geldings at the end of the list have proved unsatisfactory and are to be disposed of, probably to be replaced by the four- and five-year olds when these have been finally schooled and castrated. 'Double guelding' is an abbreviation for 'double-backed guelding' – a horse with the broad back essential for the side-saddle of the period. The 'male horse' is not a stallion. It is to be led in hand, on journeys, carrying a mail or valise with spare clothing, often known as a 'cloke bagge'. The three 'bottel horses' are used for the transport of hay and forage, measured by the bottel or bale, for the sustenance of the entire string. Possibly the stool-horse carried a portable close-stool.

Fancy names are conspicuously absent. Each horse is known by its colour and by the name of the last owner or breeder from whom the royal household acquired it either by purchase or gift. Quite possibly Grey Marcom is really Grey Markham, bred by a family of great repute as breeders and later as importers of oriental horses in the following reign. The white horse must have been bought in market overt at Smithfield, being otherwise of unknown origin. There is, significantly, only one black horse, since for reasons indicated below horses of this colour were considered unlikely to make good ladies' hacks. It is ridden by the Queen who still rode as well as any man.

Lord Mayor and Aldermen of London riding in state. (The British Library)

Performance

The ideal is expressed in terms of ability to perform certain functions, and the attributes described are about equally divided between such as will enable the animal to run up 'a hill perpendicular' (*I Henry IV*, II, iv, 339), as Douglas's did in the Border wars (utility), or to 'bound' for a lady's favour, as Henry V's did in peacetime (display of manège exercise), or with slow and stately pace to keep on his course in some such procession as Bolingbroke's triumph. By the light of copious examples from the text both of the poems and the plays we can examine Shakespeare's ideal, first equine, then equestrian.

Perhaps because by nature horsemen are a somewhat conservative breed, their terminology within the English language had failed to keep up with developments in general. Orthographically, grammatically, and in every way, the English of Henry VIII and his subjects was disorderly to the point of anarchy, lacking in uniformity and precision, uncertain of its terms of reference, neither one thing nor the other. The frame of medieval English had come apart and the structure of modern English had not yet taken shape. By contrast the English of the Elizabethans was a model of clarity, uniformity and precision. It was almost the English of the Authorized Version, which has been preserved in preference to the more chaotic versions of the scriptures current in earlier Tudor times. But the private language of horsemen still showed the imperfections of transition, and there was uncertainty as to the meaning of many of its terms. Thus even the word 'horse', most of the time, could either be singular or plural, and in the plural only could mean cavalry as well, while in the singular it could mean the species in general or the entire male specifically (as of course it often does today). But the useful and precise word 'stallion' was very rarely heard. 'Colt' did not primarily imply the male sex; one could speak of 'mare-colts' (though Shakespeare did not, and only uses the word 'filly' once in the entire works).

The hurrah-word for horse in his vocabulary was 'courser' (about a dozen instances) and as we have seen it had a history of varied meanings behind it. Originally denoting literally 'runner', in other words race-horse, a meaning it still conveyed to most of Chaucer's contemporaries, it came during the fifteenth century to be applied to the horses ridden in tournaments, and to the stately but by no means fleet horses that were ridden in progresses and processions. It is in this latter sense that the word is used by John Skelton in his poem 'On the Death of the Noble Prince, King Edward the Fourth':

> Where is now my conquest and victory?
> Where is my riches and my royal array?
> Where be my coursers and my horses high?

Another hundred years and the word had lost all technical precision.* It was used by Shakespeare to signify, primarily, the sort of horse that in the Middle Ages was known as a destrier, an armour-carrier serving in real warfare; but secondarily to signify any horse of high quality. However, since racing was still called 'coursing', whether it consisted of a match between horses or a match between greyhounds after hares, of necessity the word 'courser' was still now and again applied to race-horses.

Even the most specialised expressions of this kind were becoming so loosely used that they were all but meaningless. 'Palfrey', for instance, which everyone knew meant a pacing, ambling, easy-going saddle-horse, could sometimes be used in poetry and on the stage to signify the exact opposite, as in the celebrated and often quoted boast of the Dauphin in *King Henry V* (III, vii, 28). Here the same animal is called a courser (in the fifteenth-century sense) and a palfrey, which is manifest nonsense indulged in simply in aid of alliteration – 'prince of palfreys'. Chaucer only did this once – in *Sir Topas*, which is a deliberate burlesque. A like

---

* When works on breeding use the word 'courser' it is shorthand for 'Courser of Naples', just as they use 'jennet' as shorthand for 'Jennet of Spayne', meaning Andalusian.

degeneration appears in Shakespeare's use of the word 'steed', and many followed him along this downward path. 'Steed' was the modern form of the Anglo-Saxon word *steda* (stallion), and in the age of chivalry 'stede' was used side by side with its French equivalent *destrier* to signify a knight's first-line battle-horse (which was invariably an entire stallion). In Shakespeare's mouth it has come to mean almost any expensive saddle-horse that is not specifically a lady's ride, and that is all that was left of the masculine connotations. The word 'stallion' occurs nowhere in Shakespeare, reflecting the extreme rarity of the word in the literature of his age, though earlier and later it is common enough, from the moment when the French word *estalun* became naturalised in the twelfth century.

Conformation

Standards of perfection, for the audience as well as for the artist, tend to be regarded as universal, absolute and unchanging, and also conforming to those standards within their immediate field of observation. So also with horses, alike for Shakespeare and for the groundlings in the Southwark playhouses. The perfect horse, in their imagination, could only have the lineaments of the Spanish 'gennet' which they saw best ridden daily by the rich and powerful when they were out to impress. It is in this light that we should regard the celebrated lines in *Venus and Adonis*:

> So did this horse excel a common one,
> In shape, in courage, colour, pace and bone.
> Round-hoof'd, short-jointed, fetlocks shag and long,
> Broad breast, full eye, small head, and nostril wide,
> High crest, short ears, straight legs and passing strong,
> Thin mane, thick tail, broad buttock, tender hide:
> Look what a horse should have he did not lack,
> Save a proud rider on so proud a back.   (293–300)

Here are enumerated half of the thirty or so points which Morgan in his *Perfection* says were habitually looked for by judges of horses. Bearing in mind that the word 'small' could still bear in English the sense it had had in Chaucer's vocabulary – narrow – we should turn back to Morgan's summary of desirable points at the beginning of this chapter. There is only one striking discrepancy: in this extended description of the ideal animal *as traditionally received* Morgan describes the hoofs as 'black, smooth, dry, large, *round* and hollow'. But in another passage from his book, quoted below, he describes 'a leane deep hoove'; by 'leane' Morgan seems to imply narrow, but this might well apply only to the hindfeet, which are narrower always than the forefeet of the same animal.

The general impression given both by Morgan's and Shakespeare's catalogue of points is of the old stamp of Andalusian horse, slightly influenced by artistic standards both verbal and plastic. But as we shall see below, for more than a thousand years the European artist had been conditioned to regard the excellencies of the Iberian horse as absolute. There is little, save perhaps 'full eye', 'tender hide' and 'nostril wide', that reminds one specifically of the Turk or the Arabian, or of their scion the Thoroughbred that was yet to be born. But 'fetlocks shag and long', 'broad breast', 'high crest', 'short ears', 'thick tail', 'broad buttock' were all hallmarks of the old Andalusian sort. There is a teasing element in this whole passage because the likeness is drawn line by line and we await the moment when the artist comes to colour it with that hue in which Adonis's horse excelled. And it never comes. Why? It was probably so obvious, in this classical context, as not to be worth writing. In antiquity, divine horses were 'the colour of the sun' and this golden dun colour was also typical of the royal Cordovan stud in Andalusia. Those of the audience who were not aware of the first point would be aware of the second.

COLOUR

The position of black horses was equivocal. In general there was a demand for them at all levels of society, but they must not be totally black:

> owing
> Not a hair's worth of white – which some will say
> Weakens his price; and many will not buy
> His goodness with this note; which superstition
> Here finds allowance.   (*Two Noble Kinsmen* V, iv, 50–4)

This was the charger which reared up and fell over backwards, causing fatal injuries to Arcite, one of the Noble Kinsmen. Horses of this colour were reckoned untrustworthy for reasons on which Nicholas Morgan was almost alone in pouring scorn, at least in print. In his chapter 'Of the Colour of Horses' he names, among 'those which they *call* the best', black, full of silver hairs, and indeed any mark on a black horse would redeem it from the evil reputation which the colour enjoyed as being too sluggish and too much subject to the element of earth and the humour of melancholy. Morgan believed in the elements and the humours all right; he just did not believe that the colour of hair had anything to do with them or that a black horse was necessarily 'of the earth, then melancholy, faint-hearted and heavie, and of colour dark dun, russet or black'. In practice, however, an absolutely black horse is a great rarity and most vendors could point to a star, a blaze, a few white hairs in the forehead, or part of a white foot, which by a touch of the phlegmatic element, water, redeemed their colt from its chthonic dis-advantages. If no such mark were present, then it was the easiest thing in the world to produce a conspicuous small area of white hairs on the horse, and any farrier would be willing to oblige (most of them had quack recipes to produce this effect).

To be perfectly consistent, to act up to their beliefs, no Elizabethan who could afford the choice should have owned a white horse either, let alone bred from it. Yet not only in poetry, dramatic and otherwise, but in real life, persons of eminence appear mounted on white horses. The Queen, for instance, at the most dramatic (not to say theatrically managed) moment of her reign, made her heartening speech at Tilbury, when the Armada was off the coast, from the back of Grey Tilbury. This was despite the well-known phlegmatic, aqueous nature of all such animals, and their notorious physical and temperamental instability. However, according to one school of thought, dapple grey was among those colours in which the element of air and the sanguinary humour prevailed, making it eminently suitable for military purposes. And many dapple grey horses bleached out to pure white in late maturity. Few horses are born white: at the stud which Emperor Ferdinand I's son set up at Lipizza in 1580 all the foals were and are born black, but nearly all Lipizzans are pure white by about seven years old. The military disabilities of Richard III's White Surrey may thus have been less than skin-deep. Probably he was born black. It was really only milk-white – 'white-born' as the Germans say – steeds that were so unsuitable for hard campaigning.

Marcus Fugger, Lord of Kirschberg and Weissborn, will serve as the most articulate exponent of this theory. His *Von der Gestüterey* (Of Horse Breeding) was printed at Augsburg in 1584, and under 'White Horses' he wrote:

> The white colour in horses is like unto the element of water and such are held to be phlegmatic, fluid, indolent, and weak; they are to be used only for show, and never at need. For just as ice and snow which arise out of cold and damp have no real substance, but with a little heat melt away, so it is with horses of this colour . . .

The same mistrust of white (as opposed to grey) he applied also to parti-coloured animals, piebalds (black and white) and skewbalds (brown or bay or chestnut and white) alike, since part of them was aqueous or rheumy and one never knew *which* part, internally. Some people also extended their prejudice to the roan, in which individual white hairs are mingled with those of darker pigment, throughout the coat.

                                   ⧉ ⧉ ⧉

There is a reference to markings deemed unlucky, and hence price-reducing, in *Antony and Cleopatra*:

Aprippa: He has a cloud in's face.
Enobarbus: He were the worse for that were he a horse.   (III, ii, 51)

But as regards the colour of the coat, it is sufficiently obvious that Shakespeare did not consider this of the slightest importance. There are three mentions of roan, as noted below, and three bay horses: the one that trotted over a four-inch bridge in *Lear*, old Lord Lafeu's Curtal in *All's Well*, and the bay horse that Timon gave away in Athens. The only grey was owned by the witless Andrew Aguecheek in *Twelfth Night*. Dun occurs once, in *Romeo and Juliet*. Here the reference is so obscure that few playgoers would recognise the connection with horses at all: 'Dun's the mouse' (I, iv, 40), because mouse means favourite, and the favourite colour for cart-horses was dun, typical of tough, unkillable native stock like Exmoor. *Dun's in the mire* was a game simulating the rescue of a cart-horse from a 'slough' by plough-oxen with wainropes (for the preference of carters for dun 'capuls' see Chaucer). The only white horse is White Surrey. The only black is the one in *Two Noble Kinsmen* who are themselves of doubtful pedigree.

   This relative disregard of colour is typical of Shakespeare's practical approach to horses and horsemanship. The only practical significance of colour is as an aid to identification, as in Grey Poole and so on in the lists of the royal horses. Or else, in terms of William Shakespeare's experience in youth, or of any man in any age who has had to do his own grooming: dark-coloured horses are better than grey or white horses because they show the dirt less. Dun horses are best of all, being the colour of mud.

BREEDS

In his *Perfection of Horsemanship* (1609), Nicholas Morgan set out a table of breeds, arranged in order of popular esteem in England:

1.   Arabian
2.   Thessalian
3.   Neapolitan
4.   Barbary
5.   Turkey
6.   Spanish (Andalusian)
7.   Sardinian and Corsican
8.   Hungarian
9.   High Almaine (German, South of the Main)
10.   Flaunders
11.   Swethland (Swedish)
12.   Irish
13.   Friesian

He noted that Great Britain ranked nowhere in this order of prestige but that proverbially England excelled in palfreys, Scotland in trotting geldings (from Galloway) and 'Brittaine'' (meaning Wales) in hackneys.

Some of these assessments are purely theoretical. Thus (2) only figures so high up, or at all, because of the authority of classical antique writers. In practice there were no imports from Thessaly, and none from (7) or (11). Probably Morgan's readers would have been bitterly disappointed with the appearance of the Sardinian pony in real life. This means that in reality the Hungarian comes in sixth place. Morgan himself does not agree with this scale; he merely quotes it as a majority opinion. Before the Union of Crowns in 1603 there had been some importation of Swedish, as of Danish, horses into Scotland because of the English export ban. But all of them were stallions, so that the last of the purebred Swethlands would have died in Scotland by the end of James I's reign. The complete absence of France from this rating is interesting, specially as this list partially reflects a characteristically English form of snobbery that esteems any imported article above the native product. What is significant about this pecking order is that the list is both longer, and differently graded, than that which it is possible to extract from Blundeville's *Fower Cheifest Offyces* written early in the Queen's reign. Evidently, in the years between, English experience had widened and the taste in horseflesh had altered notably in favour of oriental and southern breeds. The horse world may look static from the internal combustion standpoint – *eppur si muove*.

As to 'native' horses, Morgan remarks on the consistently high quality and stiff prices of horses bred 'in the North parts of this kingdom'. Coming from a Welshman domiciled first in Northamptonshire and then in Kent this must be taken as an objective judgement.

If there had been no Civil War it is probable that the development which, from the equestrian point of view, is the most significant one of the seventeenth century in England would have been greatly accelerated, and England would have had an even longer start on the Continental powers in the field of horse-breeding. As it was, the military atmosphere of the 1640s and 1650s tended to slow down the transition from what was essentially a medieval scale of values in horseflesh to that prevalent in the modern era. It brought back into the limelight the warhorse, which had been losing ground in England during the years 1558–1625 when English armies were very little committed to warfare on the Continent and the cavalry establishment was kept correspondingly low. The importation of oriental horses began on a serious scale during the lifetime of Shakespeare, but nobody in England thought of them as potential warhorses or sires of such. The imports and their progeny were simply the playthings of the nobility, and when the Civil War broke out the lessons in cavalry technique demonstrated by the Thirty Years' War, then drawing to a close in Central Europe, were simply not applied in England. Chief among those lessons were that speed and mobility could only be achieved by the use of horses with oriental blood. But at the outset of the English Civil War both sides sought out troop-horses and even officers' chargers of the old heavy slow type, and as the war progressed efforts were made to breed more of the same sort, to the detriment of light-horse breeding. A partial result of the sacrifice which landowners and their tenants had made, in the cause of King or Parliament as the case might be, was that at the beginning of Cromwell's Protectorate the stock of fast light horses was less than it had been in the year of Shakespeare's death, because no Englishman thought of them in a military context.

Such progress as had been made towards the realisation of the Thoroughbred race-horse in Shakespeare's lifetime was almost entirely due to the most accessible of hot-blooded orientals, the Barb, fourth (or in reality third) on Morgan's list. It came cheaper than either the Arabian or the Turk, but was still very expensive, as may be demonstrated from the Cecil Papers. In 1610 Lord Burghley bought from Sir Robert Alexander a Great Horse, English-bred, for £100. It would be suitable for a general's charger, or as a parade horse for a civilian of equal rank – a 'great gambading horse'. In 1609 Lord Cranbourne wrote home from a continental tour that Lord Sheffield had bought a Barb horse in France for £100 f.o.b. Marseilles. By the time he got it to Paris it had 'stood him in' £140. By the same reckoning a further £20 would have to be added to the bill at Calais, then the freight to Dover. By the time the horse got to London, or a short way up-country beyond that, the total cost would be not far short of £200, or twice the price of the Alexander Great Horse. And a Barb was only suitable for sporting purposes. Despite this limited use, there were Englishmen willing to buy oriental hot-bloods, inhibited only by the price and the very few opportunities that existed for purchase, which could only be managed by favour of the Turkish authorities after the Anglo-Turkish treaty of 1580. Shipping costs were a great item. From the time of the Crusades to the end of the seventeenth century there was a constant ratio between the passenger fares and horse freights (1 horse = 2½ passengers). This was valid for all voyages except mere daylight ferrying on which the horse did not have to be fed, and made no demands on the limited water-supply. The fact that on voyages of any length deck-space was encumbered by trusses of forage (the baling-press had not been invented) was only one reason why shipmasters did not really like this cargo, and charged accordingly.

There were no English-bred Barbs, only halfbreds, since the Moors at this time never sold mares abroad, any more than the Turks or the Arabs did. Mares described as Barb or Turk or Arabian in wills of the period are only so called for reasons of prestige; everybody knew what was really meant.

Both Turkish and Arabian horses will have been noted in Morgan's table of preferred breeds above, and they had also figured in Blundeville's before that. But in practice the importation of these breeds was so infrequent that they had as yet made little impression genetically on the English light horse. The importers wanted to ride their costly acquisition or have them ridden publicly in their service, and at this time, as we have seen above (Chapter 3), breeders and their scientific advisers were all against spending a horse upon mares, for it was death's best harbinger, weakening and decaying. Thus no oriental stallion was used at stud until he was well past his best as a courser.

The Great Horse of the best quality was still what is now called the Andalusian of southern Spain, and was then called the Spanish Horse *tout court* (Morgan's no. 6) or more confusingly the genet (jennet). The Great Horse of entirely English ancestry was by comparison slow and unhandy and lacking endurance (then called 'bottom').

The only English breed that had both speed and endurance enough for racing (see Chapter 15 below) was called most often 'the breed of the North' but it was not tall enough for military or processional use. It must have been more like the Galloway to which it was allied by blood, and it had been selectively bred by monastic establishments, notably by Cistercian houses such as Fountains and Jervaulx, before the Dissolution. D'Arcy of Pontefract had reported to Cromwell, when he was winding up the Jervaulx estates, that the horses bred there were 'ever the tried breed in the North'. The following letter about a potential racehorse of this stamp, early in James I's reign, is typical.

20 Dec 1608   Selaby*

   My Lord

Whereas at my last being with your honour I promised yr. Lordship to enquire after a good horse in these parts as I thought befitting for your Lordship's purpose; these therefore are to advise you that I have been in some speeches with a very near kinsman of mine who at this instant has one of the choicest young horses that I can hear of in this country, and at my request is contented to let me have the said horse for £20 so that he may have notice from me of yr. Lordship's pleasure at or before the 2nd day of February next. Otherways the owner of the horse is purposed to put him to coursing. The horse is of colour bright bay, with a black tail and mane, a star in his forehead and a white snyp on his nose, with his near hinder foot white, now 4 yrs. old and coming 5; assuring yr. Lordship upon my word out of the credit of the owner of the horse that he is for his time the swiftest horse in these parts, and very sound of wind & limb. And for my better security of assurance to have the said horse of my said kinsman Thomas Wicliffe, I have given him the money in hand for binding of the said bargain, to whom I shall upon notice from yr. Lordship pay the said £20, which I shall be ready to receive again of yr. Honour at Candelmas term next, at which time I purpose, God willing, to come personally to do my most bounden duty to yr. Honour ... What your Lordship's pleasure is may be by yr. Letter to me returned to His

---

   * In Lower Teesdale, about halfway between Darlington ('Darnton') and Barnard Castle.

Majesty's postmaster Peter Glover at Darnton, who will presently send the same to me.

Francis Brakinbury

To Lord Cranbourne
Hatfield House, Hertfordshire

The owner Thomas Wicliffe had been in the employ of the Earl of Northumberland and his family had been tenants of one of the numerous Percy estates in North Yorkshire. Evidently the horse is by an oriental stallion out of a Cleveland Bay mare. A pure Cleveland never has such white marks.

We may note some words which make the terminology of equestrian sports so confusing at this date. 'Put him to coursing' means here put him into training as a racehorse (but 'race' then meant a stud or herd of horses). Elsewhere at the same time coursing can mean a form of hunting, as now, and more rarely a courser could still mean a horse for jousting in its last and decadent phase. Note this is only a *potential* racehorse, and it is four (coming five) years old. At the age of seven, after training and some success in 'riding wagers' it may fetch as much as £100 or the price of a good but not outstanding Great Horse. Brakinbury gives his postal address as Darnton (Darlington) and it was between there and Thirsk and Richmond that the best of these horses were being bred.

In so far as a 'native' ancestry is to be sought in the obscure ancestry of the Thoroughbred, it will probably be found among the indigenous race of horses centring in this region about Bedale, either side of the Great North Road.

◊ ◊ ◊

It has been asserted that the works of Shakespeare show such a high regard for Barb Horses that this probably reflects a personal preference of the playwright, and that indeed he probably owned a Barb. I cannot find it; 'tis not in the bond. These references consist only of two passages, barring the highly uncomplimentary mention in *Othello* (I, i, 112); one famous one at the end of *Richard II* (V, v, 78, 81) in which the captive king and his ex-groom reminisce about Roan Barbary, and the other in the last act of *Hamlet* (V, ii, 157), where the stakes on the fatal duel are six Barbary horses on the one part against six French swords on the other. One might as well say the author had a predilection for roan horses, since these are mentioned in *Richard II* and in *I Henry IV* (twice) — which is not much, but as much mention as the Barb as such is accorded. Admittedly, Roan Barbary does seem to be an invention of the author's own, since no contemporary account of Richard II's decline and fall mentions his owning a horse of that breed or colour, nor can any corroboration be found in the Wardrobe Accounts for the year 1399.

More likely the author simply thought of something expensive and fashionable in his own time, suitable for a royal personage. In fact the limitations of the Barb made it as unlikely to be used by the playwright as used, for the purpose described, by his hero. As a processional horse, whether going under Richard II or Henry IV, its speed would be wasted; nor had it in general the 'presence' or the stature required for the mobile throne: an Andalusian would have suited the part much better. In the next century Barb horses were in use as chargers for very senior officers, but by then English light cavalry worked at a faster pace than the 'horse' of the main battle in Richard's or Henry's or Elizabeth's time. It would have been of no service to a cavalry commander at any time before the Civil War to be mounted on a horse with which his fastest troops could not keep up. Its most likely military role would be to carry a dispatch rider, but hardly at the price such horses commanded. As to its potential service to the author, what little we know about his investment of the modest financial rewards of twenty-five years' work in and for the theatre makes it seem unlikely that he would have expended so much on what seems a luxury item of limited utility. Had he wished to spend so much on a status symbol, a coach would have been a likelier buy: no more expensive, and no more limited in utility – it could have carried his wife, which a Barb courser could not. The Barb was first, and almost solely at this period, a racehorse; not the proper conveyance for a late-middle-aged, middle-class ex-Londoner resettled in Stratford, a potential justice 'with eye severe, and beard of formal cut'. Nor, at the height of his London success, would a Barb have been at all suitable for a 'street nag'.

The other two oriental breeds known to English contemporaries, the Turk and the Arabian, are not mentioned at all, and the most expensive European breed, the Andalusian, only by implication (as 'jennet'). Those who classify Shakespeare as a Barb-fancier will find little comfort in the lines from *Venus and Adonis*, quoted above, which so clearly describe the Andalusian horse. But all this simply means that Shakespeare, like the majority of his countrymen, was not interested in breeds as such, only in performance. In life, as in the theatre, the top-ranking horse has its importance as a prestigious and majestic plinth for the heroic figure, or as a swift means of communication – and where its ancestors were foaled, whether in Barbary or Arabia or the lands of the Grand Turk or the Great Cham or the Sophy, is of interest only to a minority of horse-fanciers as of playgoers. The secret of commercial success in show business is to concentrate on the interests of the majority, as Shakespeare well understood.

There is a reference in *Henry VIII*, highly realistic, to the native North Country breed, when the Lord Chamberlain enters bearing a letter from the royal agent in Yorkshire, and reads: 'the horses your lordship sent for ... I saw well chosen,

Andrea del Verrocchio, mounted statue of Colleoni (1485–8) in Venice. (Photograph: Alinari)

ridden and furnish'd. They were young and handsome, and of the best breed in the north' (II, ii, 1–4). This is like an echo of D'Arcy's letter to Cromwell, written not much later than the action of the play, from the same quarter of England: 'Ever the tried breed in the North.'

THE EQUINE IDEAL IN ART

If we look at any technical, as opposed to literary, work of the period, we find the conformation of the Great Horse, which was still the prestige horse *par excellence*, summarised as follows, for instance, in Nicholas Morgan's *Perfection of Horsemanship*:

> a leane slender head, broad forehead, great black eye, full and plain over the lids, slender, thin and lean jaws, broad, thin, long and high-reared neck, the head set on to the neck so naturally as a ramme's head when he fighteth, high withers, deep broad chest and breast, his ribbes bearing out as the lid of a truncke, with an equal evenness from his chest to his flancke, lean upright pasternes, with a leane deep hoove, somewhat narrow towards the toe.

Morgan lays this down as an absolute standard of perfection for the conformation of a 'most perfect ... and excellent horse, be he young or old without any respect of colour, country, marke, whatsoever'. But as we have suggested above, these are the specifications of the Andalusian breed as it was in his day, especially the slightly overbent effect by which the Andalusian was distinguished from the other hot-blooded breeds by the set of the head on the neck, and the hooded eye.

The description agrees in most points, but differs in others, from those which appear in 'literary' sources, notably of course as re-cast by Shakespeare in *Venus and Adonis*, as we have seen. But all these descriptions, Shakespeare's not excepted, are not what has been claimed for them, a complete schedule of desirable points of the horse as dictated by the requirements and knowledge of the practical connoisseur of horseflesh. They bear the same relationship to that schedule as the horse portrayed in the Venetian equestrian statue of Bartolommeo Colleoni would bear to an actual charger suitable to carry a condottiere of the first eminence in Gattamelata's day. This famous fifteenth-century work of Andrea del Verrocchio was duly dismembered by the expert critical knacker Lt. Col. E. Duhousset, whose study of equine proportions, written at the request of professors at the École des Beaux Arts for the instruction of art students who aspired to paint horses, was published in English in 1896.* Of the horse on which Verrocchio saw fit to mount his subject, the Colonel comments on its 'lack of elegance, thickness of body, bad outlines', and quotes the criticism of the commentator Cherbuliez:

---

* Donatello's statue of Gattamelata in Padua is open to much the same criticism so far as the horse is concerned.

Statue of the Emperor Marcus Aurelius in Rome, dating from the late second century.
(Photograph: Leonnard von Matt)

I have never been able to regard this over-vaunted horse without a sort of grief.
Recollect the small magnificent head adjusted upon this enormous body, this heavy
stomach, this massive croup, these flanks buried in fat ... This melancholy horse
suffers from plethora, and has the gloomy languishing appearance imparted by
painful digestion accompanied by somnolency. There is no action, nothing to
betoken life ...   (pp. 107–8)

This criticism arises from the fact that nearly all artists of the Renaissance, and
also those of the Middle Ages who exhibit a 'classicising' tendency (including the
unknown sculptor who modelled the famous equestrian statue of Charlemagne),
have not been drawing the horse from life, even if the human subject actually sat
for them in the saddle. They have one and all been influenced by a single antique
model whose prestige was such that they could not go wrong, in their own
estimation or that of their patrons, if they simply copied the lineaments of the
charger that appears in the equestrian statue of Marcus Aurelius. There is reason
to think this was a realistic rendering of what Marcus rode in real life. But his real
life came to an end in the year 180 of our era; and the fashionable horse of
Verrocchio's day was not of the same stamp.

The same reservation applied to all 'literary' descriptions of heroic horses then
current. They derive through a long series of translations from Latin originals such
as Virgil; or if from Greek, then late Greek authors of the Roman Empire, such as

Painted in the lifetime of Shakespeare's father, Titian's portrait gives a marvellous impression of aggressive action with the Emperor riding an obviously Iberian horse. Titian, *Charles V at the Battle of Muhlberg*, 1548. (Prado Museum, Madrid. Photograph: David Manso Martin, Madrid)

Oppian who lived in the Roman province of Syria in the second century A.D. They are essentially paraphrases of imitations and imitations of paraphrases of works that in the antique world had some immediacy, some point of contact with the horse of flesh and blood in its habit as it lived, *then*. But European horses of the fifteenth, sixteenth and seventeenth centuries had been bred for another purpose, and to a great extent from other stock, than those present in the eye of the artist in bronze or stone or words between the time of Homer and the fall of Rome. The kind of aristocratic art patron who excels at horsemanship was, and is, liable to be as conservative in aesthetic as in political views: the artist for his daily bread must please the patron, and this can best be achieved by depicting the patron's prized property not so much in terms of current standards of excellence as by those which the patron may be persuaded are 'eternal' because sanctified by the best classical usage. Veracity in terms of literal resemblance to the subject is therefore nowhere in this kind of heroic portraiture.

This timeless, derivative picture of the 'noble' horse in all media, both visual and verbal, persists in Britain and in most European countries down to sometime in the eighteenth century. It stops in Britain first, early in the century, because of that characteristic English phenomenon, the realistic *animalier* or sporting artist, who from the days of Francis Barlow (1626–1724) onwards began to depict the horse as he actually saw him. In the age of Shakespeare, however, it is only the occasional 'primitive', the unsophisticated painter or draughtsman, who shows us what he actually sees.

The one connecting link between the horses described by antique authors and sculpted by antique artists and those ridden by the upper class of Shakespearian England was breeding. Both were of the race known in antiquity as Iberian and in our day as Andalusian or Lusitano. Having been the mounts of Roman consuls in their military capacity this breed continued to be the prestige horse of all Europe until long after Shakespeare's time. For instance, no general of Marlborough's generation would be seen dead on anything else but an Andalusian stallion. But the lineaments and conformation even of this breed were not immutable over the centuries. The typical Andalusian today does not look *quite* like the horses Velázquez painted with such masterly skill ridden by Philip IV and his grandees, or those that Anthony Van Dyck took for his models when painting the English royal family: 300 years or maybe thirty horse generations, sire and dam, have brought some changes. How much more in the sixteen centuries and the 160 generations of horses that stretch from Virgil's *Georgics* to *Venus and Adonis*? Enough to make a description of a 'noble' horse derived by the one from the other at once stereotyped and untrue.*

---

* A compendium of Greek veterinary texts translated by Jean du Reuil and published at Basel under the title *Veterinariae Medicinae libri duo* in the mid-sixteenth century is typical of the channels through which a literate Englishman with a grammar-school education – that is, understanding Latin well but having only a smattering of Greek – could have absorbed point by point and accepted without question as eternally valid (because 'classic') the standards of equine *extérieur* current in late antiquity. But now that it is the lot of the Latinist, as before him of the Hellenist, to be herded into a corral labelled 'Specialists Only', the following extract of Joannes Ruellius' translation is accompanied by an English version.

　　Qualis futurus sit equus e pullo a corporis forma et indole coniectari potest; hoc vero habitu constabit. Exiguo capite, nigris oculis, naribus non angustis, brevibus auriculis et arrectis, cervice molli, densa iuba, crispiore et per dextram partem profusa, lato et musculorum toris numeroso pectore, grandibus humeris, scapulis latis, cruribus rectis, ventre substricto, testibus exiguis, spina maxime duplici, si minus curva, caude longa et setosa crispaque, rotundis clunibus, foeminibus torosis, tereti genu neque introrsus spectanti, rotundis ungulis, aequalibus, duris, quibus mediocres coronae superpositae sunt. Haec sunt futuri sublimis et bene compositi corporis iudicia.

It is possible to forecast what sort of horse a colt will grow into by the shape and quality of the body; indeed, its nature will not change. Small head, black eye, nostrils which are not narrow, short ears which stand erect,

THE IDEAL HORSEMAN

The ideal in horsemanship had nothing to do with efficient performance at those multifarious peaceful activities that could only be discharged effectively on horseback. It was assumed as a matter of course that a man of the appropriate calling would be competent for this. Nor had it much to do with military service, though fine horsemanship had a certain relationship to warlike horsemanship. It had nothing to do with hunting, still less with racing. It had everything to do with display, with 'magnificence', with what the modern show judge calls 'presence' in horse and rider. It was above all theatrical and its presentation either to a select audience of the Prince and his court or less frequently to the eyes of the vulgar had so much in common with dramatic spectacle that it is no wonder that the writers for the stage were drawn time and again to a description of it.

This exalted being could not be produced cheaply. His training required a riding barn to be erected and equipped with pillars and other adjuncts of the manège. At Petworth in 1632 this equipment came to the quite incredible sum, taking the 'mountaynes, pannel planckes and other lumberment' together, of £100. And it was all second-hand lumberment. You could build a house for that money.

  I have excluded the two most conspicuously skilful horsemen in Shakespeare from this chapter on equitation as an art. Harry Percy is mentioned in Chapter 14 below on war. His namesake Prince Hal, like him, practised horsemanship to a fine point, but with an ulterior purpose in view. What a pity we never

> ... saw young Harry with his beaver on,
> His cushes on his thighs, gallantly arm'd,
> Rise from the ground like feather'd Mercury,
> And vaulted with such ease into his seat
> As if an angel dropp'd down from the clouds
> To turn and wind a fiery Pegasus,
> And witch the world with noble horsemanship.
>
> (*I Henry IV* IV, i, 104–10)

---

smooth neck, a dense, rather curly mane which falls abundantly on the right side, a broad breast with many knots of muscles, high wither, broad shoulder-blades, straight legs, belly tucked up, small genitals, 'double' back [i.e. muscles prominent either side of the spine] which is not too dipped, a long, silken and curly tail, rounded quarters, well-muscled gaskins, smooth knees which do not turn inwards to the beholder, round, smooth and hard hoofs, with pasterns of medium length above them. These are the signs of what will be a sublime and well-built body.

Though we can see displays of vaulting in any circus in Europe, we can no longer see it done in full armour including the cushes or cuisses that encased and encumbered the thighs. But it could still be done, and was still being taught, after the Civil War, in *The Vaulting Master*, a 1641 handbook with explanatory woodcuts which was republished in 1652. The same Prince Hal, grown into King Henry V, speaks in the play of the name of 'vaulting into my saddle with my armour on my back' (V, ii, 139). Again in *Macbeth*:

> I have no spur
> To prick the sides of my intent, but only
> Vaulting ambition, which o'er leaps itself
> And falls on th'other.   (I, vii, 25–8)

If the vaulter overdoes it, he will miss the saddle entirely. But the only circus act mentioned in any of the plays and involving horses does not require the use of a rosinback. It was performed by Marocco, a horse trained by the seventeenth-century showman Mr Bankes and well-hated by actors because he kept them out of the theatre. Shakespeare could not even bring himself to utter his baneful name, in *Love's Labour's Lost*:

> How easy it is to put years to the word three ... the dancing horse will tell you.
>   (I, ii, 49)

Snaffle-riding has no ideal aspect, there is no element of display about it, and the object of those who practise it is to conserve energy rather than expend it, and so not surprisingly the plays mention it several times as part of everyday life, as in *Much Ado* for instance, when Benedick says: 'Sir, your wit ambles well; it goes easily' (V, i, 156). And in *Antony and Cleopatra*:

> The third o' the world is yours, which with a snaffle
> You may pace easy ...   (II, ii, 63–4)

Purposeless horsemanship was exemplified in the tourney, which was still part of an unbroken tradition, not a conscious antiquarian revival, in the lifetime of Shakespeare. But it was fading away, or rather was being gradually transmuted into pure equestrian displays like the carousels and ballets on horseback that later became the delight of the French court. In *Love's Labour's Lost*, Boyet says:

> Full merrily
> Hath this brave manage, this career, been run.   (V, ii, 481–2)

We should hardly know that he is speaking of the tourney and not of the High School, in which both *career* and *manage* were terms of the art, but for Berowne countering with 'Lo! he is tilting straight.' In *As You Like It* we have 'a puisny tilter that spurs his horse but on one side breaks his staff like a noble goose' (III, iv, 39).

The object now is only to break the staff elegantly, not upset or kill the adversary. What these latter-day tournaments were like we see in *Pericles, Prince of Tyre* (II, ii), with its elaborate setting of 'A Public Way leading to the Lists. A Pavilion near it'. It is much more like a pageant than anything else, with its allegorical devices displayed on shields. And part of its *raison-d'être* appears in scene iii, the *après-joust*: a banquet prepared in a hall of state. Nobody, in the second scene, comments on the robustness of the knight, the deadly qualities of his weapons, the aptness of his horse for knocking his opponents head over heels, as they might do in a similar passage by Chaucer, say. That is not what they have come for. What they have been to see is horsemanship as art, and this will be dealt with in the next chapter.

8

Horsemanship as an art

As art united with experience long
Taught him those lofty steeds in awe to hold.

Thus wrote Nicholas Morgan in his obituary on Sir Robert Alexander, Kt, of Walton-on-Thames, who in 1588–9 was Gentleman Rider to the Earl of Northumberland and later Equerry of the Stable to the Queen herself, until his death in 1609. 'Not only he in England was esteemed,' says Morgan, 'but eke in foreigne countries for his art', thereby implying that Sir Robert was an English horseman of international repute – as it might be today a dressage exponent of Olympic standard. Alas for Morgan's patriotic implications. Not only is the name of Robert Alexander nowhere to be found in Continental writings on the High School, then or later, but neither is it the real name of this hero, who was born Roberto Zinzano. He was just another Neapolitan riding-master, though he had three English-born sons.

Morgan wrote his book after retiring from legal practice, near Sevenoaks in Kent, and must have been born about 1550. His is the first generation of English writers to think, as a matter of course, of horsemanship as an art. It is noticeable, among treatises on horsemanship, that the tone of the Introductions, Dedications, Prefaces, Forewords, Commendations, and all other preliminaries becomes more rarified, and their extent greater, until they culminate in those prefixing the Duke of Newcastle's classic treatise *A General System of Horsemanship* (1658), in reading which one wonders if he is ever going to cut the cackle and come to the horses.

Yet the more desperate and the more long-winded their efforts to define the means whereto horsemanship is an end, the more they convince the reader that the justification is not needed, and that the writers know this in their hearts. Once horsemanship has attained the status of an art, it automatically becomes an end in itself. No one enquires into the purposes of a statue by Donatello, because they are so obviously twofold: first, to exist in all its perfection, and second, to keep the artist alive. In this field there existed, in the day of Shakespeare, the professional side by side with the amateur. The latter was engaged in raising what had been one of the accomplishments of a gentleman, which enabled him to discharge effectively the functions appropriate to his station, to the status of those skills practised by the Renaissance aesthetic superman – another *virtù*. Newcastle was to be the prime English example. But a professional like Zinzano could do moderately well for himself. With the Percies he earned £10 a year in cash, a very superior bed and board at Petworth, and a handsome clothing allowance. In the royal establishment at Windsor his regular emoluments in cash and kind were not much better, but then there was the knighthood, and the fringe benefits would be a shade higher. His eldest son and successor in office, Sir Robert junior, was in the habit of selling Great Horses ready-made for £100 each; and of course they had been 'made' in the King's time.

For a great many ordinary purposes (ordinary, that is, in the life of a landowner) the old 'country' style of equitation – 'snaffle-riding' – would serve very well: for travel, for hunting, for hawking. The essentially military style, practised on the Great Horse, did not need to be brought to that pitch of perfection demanded by the academic riding-master for the rider to be the terror of the Queen's enemies. Notoriously, Napoleon's seat on a horse would have brought tears to the eyes of every *écuyer-professeur* in Europe, but he seems to have got along all right. Yet the apologist for the art of riding in Shakespeare's day always made great play with the military obligations of the equestrian class. If the object had really been the making of more effective soldiers, then surely horsemanship at that level would have been taught in closer partnership with skill-at-arms; whereas the only weapon used in those equestrian exercises into which the tourney finally degenerated – running at the ring, and the like – was the lance. And the lance had ceased to be a decisive factor in mounted warfare. If the gambades and the bounds, which cost so much painstaking time to teach the horse, were justified in terms of their utility in close combat, why were they not practised in concert with swordsmanship? Why were there no competitions in loading a pistol while one's horse did the levade, or firing it while he executed a capriole?

The answer is that the military side of it was really an elaborate pretence. What had grown out of the military side of feudal service now derived from one alone of the three obligations by which a knight in England had held his fee. Field service

A halfe Canon with a broken port, ioined with one plight within another.

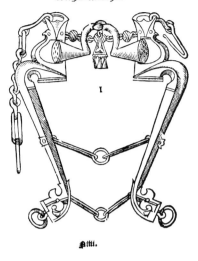

I

Aliii.

A Bastonet or Iesue bit, with two turning buttons.

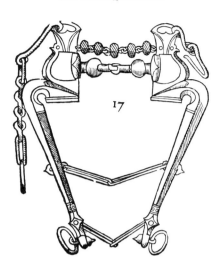

17

A Canon with an vpset mouth complete, and ioined with a peece.

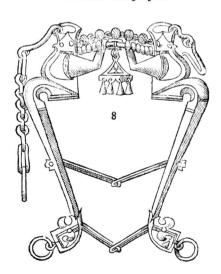

8

A halfe Canon with an vpset mouth, hauing trenches aboue.

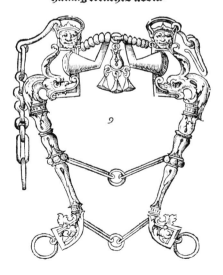

9

A Scatch with a whole port.

A whole port with Oliues.

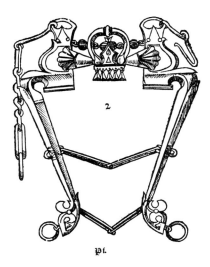

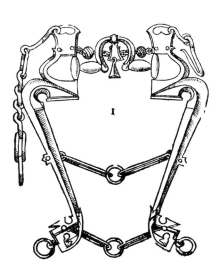

A halfe Scatch with a broken port ioined with one plight within another.

A halfe Scatch with a broken port, ioined with a riuet naile.

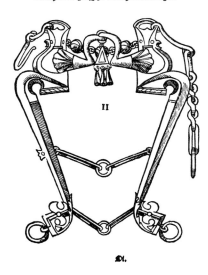

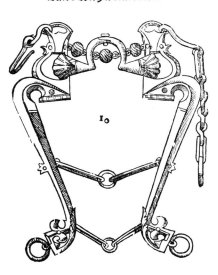

Stubborn bits illustrated in Blundeville, *The Fower Cheifest Offyces of Horsemanship*, after Grisone. (By permission of the Syndics of Cambridge University Library)

for forty-two days in the year was gone for ever. So was castle-guard; but the third service, *equitatio* or *chevauchée*, the obligatory mounted escorting of the overlord from one end of the vassal's estates to the other, still had its counterpart so long as the court progressed from one provincial palace to another at seasonal intervals. And the court did not become utterly static until well on in James I's reign. In order that all manner of subjects might be duly impressed with the monarch's majesty, the noblemen and gentlemen of the royal train must make a brave show on horseback.

To this extent the aristocrat who wished to play a part in court life must be able and willing to play his part in putting on a show. And for the better performance of this professional style of horsemanship as well as for the kind of mounted ballet or carousel into which the last relics of the tourney finally merged, the services of foreign (in practice almost exclusively Italian and French) riding-masters were retained. Not only did they train adult pupils in equitation, they also 'made' suitable horses for this special function.

The aspiration to excel in this exercise was such an enormous commitment that, in the context of post-Renaissance court life, it would seem trifling to allow that what one was spending, or had spent, so much time, trouble and treasure in learning was anything less than an art. After all, a certain kind of swordplay was called 'the art of fence'. It had little to do with ordinary fighting as practised on the battlefield: it was taught almost exclusively by foreigners; it could only be practised under artificial and circumscribed conditions; and an ordinarily competent *maître d'armes* could probably teach his pupil to wield the rapier up to an acceptable standard in a quarter the time which his colleague would need to school the same pupil *and his horse* to the corresponding standard. Morgan asks:

> How then shall it be possible, for a gentleman to attain perfection, in so honour-able and difficult an art as Horsemanship, without many years' study and practice, whenas all Kings, Princes, and Nobilitie become schollers for many yeares, only to attain to ride well (being but a particular part of horsemanship)?

Of course it was not possible, and perhaps this rather transcendental quality was what attracted the real *aficionados*. However well one performed it was theoreti-cally possible to do even better. Equitation had then, and has still, a hard core of devotees whose goal is none other than Morgan's 'perfection' which they know to be unattainable, and that is what made it an art, and not a craft. Which also means, automatically, that even the most near-perfect performance could not be of any conceivable *use*, for an ulterior purpose. But horsemanship does not appear to have reached this philosophical dead-end until after the lifetime of Shakespeare.

those that tame wild horses
Pace 'em not in their hands to make 'em gentle,
But stop their mouths with stubborn bits and spur 'em,
Till they obey the manage.   (*Henry VIII* V, ii, 55–8)

We should not read too much into the word 'wild'. It was the usual term for unbroken horses, especially those that had been bred on the common grazings or in parks, and had never been handled between the time they were rounded up and branded in their first autumn and the day when they were taken up for breaking four years later. The word had been in use in this sense since before the Norman Conquest, and is to be found in Old English wills and charters where the stock of certain estates is said to include so many 'wilde mearas' or 'equae silvaticae'. With this reservation, the speech by Gardiner quoted above will serve very well as a reference to the two branches of horsemanship. 'Pace 'em not in their hands' describes the education of the horse in the old 'snaffle-riding' fashion, and it might even be read to mean that nursery-schooling which William Browne recommended for pacing horses, while they were still very young foals.

The stubborn bits, those fearsome curbs illustrated in the woodcuts to works like those of Frederigo Grisone and his English disciples, were part of the equipment for making the Great Horse, and these two lines describe the way that things were done in the best stables in Henry VIII's time, though no longer when Shakespeare wrote his play about Henry VIII. Just by accident, the author has got the period detail right for once. No doubt the 'stubborn' method was still being practised in the lifetime of Roberto Zinzano and Mr Parise and Mr Westcott who served under him at Petworth, but not by such as them. It was quicker, and thus cheaper, but the product was inferior. A great deal more time and patience were now bestowed on the making of the Great Horse; the expert did not begin with a 'wild' horse, but one that had already been mouthed and backed and was accustomed to handling and to civilised behaviour in a stable.

Harry Hotspur, whose feats of horsemanship will be noted elsewhere, did not practise equitation as an art, nor did that loquacious windbag the Dauphin; both, in their different ways, used it as an ancillary technique for their style of fighting. In *Hamlet* the Frenchman Lamord, whom we do not actually see, is much more typical of the dedicated exponent of the art for its own sake:

Here was a gentleman of Normandy—
I have seen myself, and serv'd against, the French,

> And they can well on horseback, but this gallant
> Had witchcraft in't. He grew unto his seat,
> And to such wondrous doing brought his horse
> As he had been incorps'd or demi-natur'd
> With the brave beast.   (IV, vii, 81–7)

This Norman was mentioned almost in the same breath with Laertes' prowess as a 'scrimer' (fencer), and there were people about courts who lived for sword-play. Osric was one, but like Laertes himself what he enjoyed was the exercise of skill and agility with the foils. There were others, caricatured by Touchstone in *As You Like It*, who were willing to fight with naked points at the drop of a hat, and these psychopathic compulsive swordsmen were a menace in any prince's train. By contrast, the hippomania of such as the Neapolitan Prince in *The Merchant of Venice* was very harmless.

   As to the professional nagsmen retained by great houses, they are mentioned with some bitterness by Orlando, speaking of his mean brother:

> His horses are bred better; for besides that they are fair with their feeding, they are taught their manage, and to that end riders dearly hired.   (*As You Like It* I, i, 10).

In passing we may note a change of usage in the word 'bred'. Here Orlando certainly does not mean what a modern speaker would imply by 'better bred' horses – animals of superior pedigree – but only better kept horses. *Fair* with their feeding indicates the conditions in which they were kept for the manage. For once, 'fair' is divorced from its almost invariable complement: the expression 'fat and fair' is much more common, and any contemporary picture of horses from an upper-class stable shows them in much more abundant flesh than would be deemed suitable nowadays. A slimmer outline for the high-class horse did not come in until well on in Charles II's time, due to the influence of racehorse training which combined copious feeding with the most rigorous sweating and purging. We have seen above what 'dearly hired' amounted to – about £10 a year, all found, with perquisites.

   Like all upper-class pastimes such as hunting, hawking and heraldry, the art of riding had its own vocabulary, largely at this period French and Italian in origin. Familiarity with it, if not the practice of the art itself, was the touchstone of fashionable people. Thus Celia's 'Cry holla to thy tongue, I prithee; it curvets unseasonably' (*As You Like It* III, ii, 240), is here correctly used. Such were the 'terms of manage' that Hotspur spoke in his sleep to his bounding steed (*I Henry IV* II, iii, 50), constantly in the mouths of those who, like Henry V, would bound their horses for a lady's favour, and sit like a jackanapes, never off. We may indeed point here to an ulterior motive for learning the art, but equitation is not the only art that has been practised then and since to gain a lady's favour. Nevertheless there were enough instances where the motive was purely aesthetic, simply to produce something beautiful, in four dimensions of which the fourth was motion, never more tellingly described than in *Pericles, Prince of Tyre*:

> a courser whose delightful steps
> Shall make the gazer joy to see him tread.   (II, i, 157–8)

9

Sickness and injury

The generation of 1588–1613 was at risk, so far as its horses and much else were concerned, from a hazard which for ours does not exist. It is a long time since we said farewell to rewards and fairies, and to the witch with them. But the subjects of Elizabeth, and still more those of James I, had to reckon with a whole category of setbacks in the stable ranging from disaster to mere inconvenience, caused by the operation of witchcraft. At the worst, we may look to the records of the trial at Chelmsford in 1579 of Margery Stanton, accused of bewitching to death 'One white gelding valued at £3 and one cow valued at forty shillings.' In this case the jury was not satisfied with the prosecution evidence, and Margery was discharged. But many were hanged or burnt for similar offences on no better evidence.

'Ill-wishing' a horse might, according to the current belief, have two effects. Either it might die of a wasting disease, or it might stumble when at work, thereby causing injury to the rider or driver. Witchcraft could also induce barrenness in a mare, impotence in a stallion, or without causing outright death or injury could cast an ill-defined blight on youngstock so that they did not 'do' well.

The most trusted treatment was prophylactic. The accepted method of making safe the stable against intrusion by witches was to place a sprig of mountain ash (rowan, witchwood) over the door. Other measures such as the invocation of saints, most often St George, were much in favour, Reformation or no Reformation. No doubt witch-proofing of a whole field or 'horse close' would be more difficult, and the most frequent nuisance, the borrowing of horses by witches for nocturnal rides to their sabbats, could hardly be prevented even by the most careful owner. The infallible sign that this had been done was the finding of the

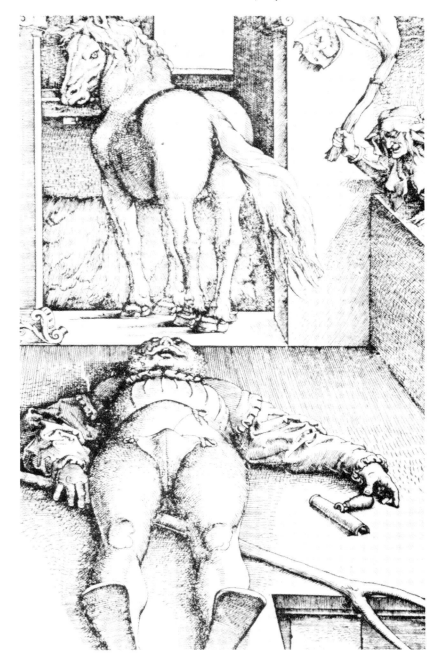

A sprig of rowan tree over the stable door would have prevented this. Hans Baldung, *Sleeping Stable Boy and Witch*, woodcut, 1544. (Kupferstichkabinet of the Kunstmuseum, Basel)

horse in a sweat in the morning, and even more the state of his mane, matted and twisted into 'elf-locks' or 'witch-knots'. Devils, the masters of witches, might also exert their baleful influence. Thus in Ben Jonson's *The Devil is an Asse* (1616) Satan says patronisingly to a minor demon:

> Or crossing of a market-woman's mare,
> 'Twixt this and Tottenham? these were wont to be
> Your main achievements, Pug.   (I, i, 10–12)

Lameness might, in the absence of obvious external injury, also be diagnosed as the work of witches. Treatment of such injuries themselves was useless. The only thing to do was to get at the cause, the particular witch who had worked a spell on the horse, and employ some counter-magic which would compel her to take the spell off. This was beyond the power of any layman, and recourse must be had to a 'wiseman' who was so often capable of identifying, without aid from the owner, the witch responsible, and always of neutralising her spells by 'white' counter-spells.

Another side-effect of the prevalence of witches does not come under the heading of sickness or injury but must have caused much embarrassment to some horsemen at this time. In all the voluminous legal records relating to trials for witchcraft there is no definition of the legal liabilities of the owner of a horse which turned out to be the devil. This was not a very common occurrence and seems to have been quite unknown in the London area and the region of Warwickshire, thus coming outside the range of Shakespeare's personal experience, but there are several extant accounts of witch trials in Scotland and the North of England in which the devil who presided over the orgies of witch covens had the form of 'ane blak galoway' (pony) instead of the more conventional billygoat.

Treatment for injury and ailment arising from natural causes fell under three heads. Of these, paradoxically, the most practical had a slight aura of the supernatural about them, shading off imperceptibly into the practice of white or beneficent witchcraft. An example is the treatment for various ailments of the legs below the knee, and of the feet, which consisted of standing the horse in running water, *facing upstream*. This goes back in continuous tradition to the old leechdoms of Saxon times. No doubt in pagan times it owed much of its potency to the magical properties of running water and the benevolent influence of those water spirits, nixies and the like, which are part of the legacy of Celtic belief; then it had been important to face the horse upstream, looking towards the source where the Spirit of the Waters lived. But in practice it is virtually impossible to stand a horse in running water any other way, since its instinct is always to stand, wade or swim against the current. The efficacy of this treatment can be proved today in cases of inflamed tendons, or of laminitis, still sometimes known as 'founder' or 'fever of the feet'.

'Scientific' treatment depended on two systems, not entirely reconcilable with each other, but both logical inasmuch as they applied equally and in the same way to veterinary and medical practice. Both affected the theory, though perhaps not so much the practice, of horse-breeding. The more important was the four-element theory of the humours which went back to Hippocrates and perhaps earlier physicians. This conception of a balance of sanguinary, melancholic, choleric and phlegmatic humours, which could be upset by the preponderance of any one of them, applied also to diet. Different foods had qualities corresponding to the four elements/humours: thus high-protein feed, such as beans, still called in popular stable parlance 'heating', belonged to the choleric or fiery category.

The second 'learned' influence on horse-doctoring contained, like the first, a strong oriental element. The doctrines of classical antiquity had once come down to the English as to all the nations of the West partly through an unbroken Western channel of succession, the mouth of which was firmly stopped when the last of the scholars who had fled after Constantinople fell to the Turks had imparted all he knew and the last of his precious manuscripts had been copied or printed. But a great many works of classical antiquity, especially those on natural science, had been translated into Arabic during the great days of Islamic expansion in the Mediterranean and had been very widely diffused throughout the Muslim world. Thus the beliefs of the Elizabethans about the natural history of the horse differed not at all in principle, and very little in detail, from those expressed in books like the *Qābūs nāma* written by the Persian Kaikā'ūs in the year 1080. The reason was not identity of clinical or practical experience but derivation of theory from the same, ultimately metaphysical, antique source.

More obviously oriental than 'classical' medicine was the respectable science of astrology, with its Persian, ultimately Indian and Babylonian, origins and its technical terms borrowed from Arabic. This too, could be invoked in veterinary theory, as in human medicine. As an aid to diagnosis the hour and the place of birth of the patient had to be known. If the horse were not imported this was not so difficult as might be supposed. The foaling of top-class mares, if not actually witnessed, would be reported by the stud-groom within a matter of minutes. Since the pressures of the Thoroughbred industry which nowadays cause foals to be born in January, February and March were not then operative, most of them were born in April, May and June, when nights are short; as mares very rarely foal in daylight, the probable limits of day and hour, if not exactly known, were narrow in any case. Prognosis of an ailment in horse or man depended on how long a conjunction of the planets unfavourable to a patient born under a certain sign would continue.

Reconciliation of this system with that of the humours was less easy than making the latter square with traditional remedies. For instance, the water therapy for laminitis mentioned above could be justified on the grounds that one cause of this crippling ailment was what is now called excess of protein in the diet – in the old terminology 'heating' foods – leading to a choleric surfeit, which could be countered by submitting the patient to the influence of the phlegmatic element, water: running water because a horse runs. Q.E.D. Justification on astrological grounds no doubt required a more subtle line of ratiocination, but it could be done.

The easiest way, as it was thought, to achieve the right balance or 'temperature' between the four humours was by subtracting from those that were in excess rather than by adding to those that were wanting. Human patients suffered directly from the various eliminatory treatments, but horses at least were spared some of them. Being physically incapable of the act of vomiting, they rarely came in for the exhausting regime of emetics to which their masters were exposed, but there were hopeful practitioners who would attempt even this means of elimination. The recommended treatment to make a horse void 'foul humours' by mouth was one or two large roots of polypodium of the oak, well scraped and soaked in oil of spike overnight, then tied to the bit and the horse ridden two miles or so, fasting, in the morning. The resultant copious salivation, if not actual vomiting, ensured that at least something harmful had been voided by every possible orifice.

But they came in for the rest in full measure: bleedings, cuppings, diuretics, purgatives and all. The most desired proportion in horses was preponderance of the hot and dry, the qualities of fire and air, and this to a certain extent was sought by food additives, all with strong flavours, including ginger, pepper and garlic. But as most of these implied the use of expensive imported spices, they would have been sparingly used outside the stables of the rich.

Internal parasite

The Elizabethans lumped all these bugbears of the horsekeeper together as 'bots', a term which included everything from the subcutaneous warble-fly larva to the lung-worms and round-worms and tape-worms. Infestation was treated in the same way for all of them alike, except for what is still called 'bot', the warble-fly, for the removal of which by surgical intervention many veterinary notes of the time give directions. Otherwise there were several different remedies against 'the bots', but though the prescriptions differ in composition, none of them is intended to combat any particular species of parasite, and none of them seems likely to have been effective. Not even the turpentine–linseed drench, messy but still effective and widely used in the 1950s, was known in the 1590s. Perhaps those Elizabethan remedies which contained an infusion of broom-leaves were of some benefit.

Farrier drenching a horse. Woodcut from Fugger, *Von der Gestüterey*, 1584. (Reproduced by permission of Miland Publishers, Nieuwkoop, Netherlands)

Only Nicholas Morgan seems to distinguish between 'wormes', as follows: 'the worme, the bot, the truncheon ... they are engendered of raw and evill humours'. By truncheons he seems to mean round-worm (strongyle). He recommended this course for disinfestation: first day, give a quart of new milk, and half a pint of honey in it, to keep the worms quiet; second day, give a drench, in a quart of strong ale, of ¼ lb of fern (seed), ½ lb of savin, ½ lb of stonecrop, 2 spoonsful of brimstone, 2 spoonsful of chimney soot, steeped two hours and strained; third day, give six purging pills made of 1 lb of lard, 3 oz each of liquorice, aniseed, fenugreek, 2 oz of alloes, 1 oz of agaric, made up into 4½ oz pills, and administer them, three in the morning and three at night, in the following manner: 'catch hold of his tongue, hold it fast until you have hurled one in, and thrust it down his throat with a rowling pin'. For the next three days the horse is to have nothing but mashes and warm water. He notes that some men dose their horses with chickens' guts, 'which being a pleasanter feed than the horse maw' the 'bots' will feed on that, and with luck will be passed out with it. He stresses that no known medicine will kill worms, bots or truncheons, but only make their intestinal environment so unpleasant that they will 'flee' it, *per anum*.

The mourning of the chine

'Mourning' was the most dreaded of all ailments not involving lameness, and seems to have been identical with what we now call strangles. This is a sort of equine mumps with a continual discharge from one or both nostrils and the formation of abscesses in the angle of the jaw, which in some cases come to a head very rapidly, bursting either externally or internally. If the disease does not run its course quickly, wasting occurs because the throat is so sore that there is difficulty in swallowing. Elizabethan theory ascribed this disease to an internal rotting of the flesh along the spinal cord, the resultant pus issuing through the head. Losses were frequent because the nature of the disease was not recognised, and in particular the manner in which it was communicated by droplet infection. None of the treatments recommended in contemporary farriery notes even mentions isolation, or any measures to bring the abscesses to a head by fomentation.

A rheum or cold in the head, which might be an early stage of the dreaded 'mourning', was treated by soaking two goose feathers in oil of bay and sewing the butts to the headstall, and fastening polypodium of the oak to the bit. A hood was then put overall, and the horse ridden, fasting – as for an 'emetic' – every morning. Afterwards, in the stable, it was made to inhale the smoke of frankincense.

Glanders, which was thought to be associated in some way with strangles, was treated with poultices under the jaw among other measures, and owing to the inability of most farriers to distinguish between the two complaints a certain number of cases of 'mourning' will have benefited by this treatment.

☙ ☙ ☙

There is no instance in Shakespeare of a veterinary practitioner (horse-marshal) at work, but plenty of reference to equine ills, the witch-borne included. The hags in *Macbeth* confine their attentions among livestock to swine; but Mab, Queen of the Fairies, is indistinguishable, in mythology, from Hecate, Queen of Witches. She is the original Night-mare, and Mercutio tells us what she does to horses; she

> ... plaits the manes of horses in the night
> And bakes the elf-locks in foul sluttish hairs,
> Which, once untangled, much misfortune bodes.
>
> *(Romeo & Juliet* I, iv, 89–91)

Minor rustic demons get up to no good with horses, as Puck suggests:

> When I a fat and bean-fed horse beguile,
> Neighing in likeness of a filly foal ...
>
> *(Midsummer Night's Dream* II, i, 45)

We have seen elsewhere that the fattest horses were usually those used entirely for breeding. Any amount of rural trouble could be caused by simulating a filly on heat to entice the stallion out of his paddock at night.

To see the Elizabethan horse-doctor in action you must consult Ben Jonson among playwrights; enquire at *Bartholomew Fair*. Some of the troubles he had to cope with are listed in *The Taming of the Shrew*:

> his horse hipped ... possessed with the glanders and like to mose in the chine [the dreaded '*mourning*', perhaps], troubled with the lampass, infected with the fashions, full of windgalls, sped with spavins, rayed with the yellows [jaundice], past cure of the fives [probably a misprint for hives, but perhaps French *avives* (parotitis)], stark spoiled with the staggers, begnawn with the bots, swayed in the back and shoulder-shotten ...   (III, ii, 46)

There is nothing the Camden Town or Edinburgh graduate of today can do about a sway-back or a shotten shoulder, but cures were and are available for most of the other conditions in that list, as well as for those that Sands observed in France:

> one would take it,
> That never saw 'em pace before, the spavin,
> Or springhalt reign'd among 'em.   *(Henry VIII* I, iii, 11)

Springhalt is now called stringhalt. The spavin was of at least three kinds, according to contemporary diagnosis: wet, dry or bone. All were treated by firing with hot irons in different ways, as was a 'hipped' horse (now called 'hip down', that is, having fractured the point of the hip). External applications were of various kinds, but whatever the pharmaceutical contents of the unguents, most of them were mixed either with lard or butter for ease of spreading, and this is why the Cockney's brother in *Lear*

> in pure kindness to his horse, buttered his hay.   (II, iv, 126)

Internal medicament was either by means of pills (balls) or drenches, the latter administered per cow's horn. The Prince in *I Henry IV* makes Hotspur say 'give my roan horse a drench' (II, iv, 104).

10

Saddlery, dress and accoutrements of horse and rider

'Harness' is a shibboleth in the equestrian world of the neo-Elizabethans. To them it means exclusively the gear for attaching horses to a vehicle. In the reign of the first Elizabeth it meant that, sometimes, but much else also. It could still mean armour. It could also mean a purely decorative arrangement of straps before and behind the saddle, used on 'horses of state', such as the 'Whyte harness of whyte silke and silver, bot. the 13th of July, 1586 of Mr Richardson, 56/8d' in the accounts of the Earl of Northumberland. Such caparisons went with a saddle like the military model but elaborately tooled, chased and inlaid, a bridle infinitely scalloped and embossed, the headband adorned with 'estridge' plumes like the aigrettes worn now by circus horses and such as can be seen on the heads of chariot horses in ancient Egyptian and Assyrian pictures, the purpose being to make the horse look taller. Plain coach harness in the 1580s cost only £1 a set.

But enormous sums were expended on parade saddlery, as we can see from the Cecil Papers. Four Great Horses given to the King of Denmark in 1605, three years after *Hamlet* was written, were equipped with saddle-cloths using

29 yards of velvet at 50s	£72 10 0
Silk Lace & Fringe	£64 0 0
Saddler making up cloths	£ 7 18 4
	£144 8 4

This is £36 each without the saddles. These horses being Great Horses would have been worth upwards of £100 each, but something less than £200. The saddles, of

Princess Anne of Denmark. If all the accoutrements of the Royal House were like this, the high cost of the materials which went into them is understandable. (Reproduced by courtesy of the Trustees of the British Museum)

good utility quality, would have cost £10 or so each, though more if chased and tooled. But £10 would suffice to buy a horse that was an acceptable present from Lord Cecil to Archie, the King's influential Fool, in 1610.

All riding saddles had thick rolls before and behind the rider's leg, but the high wooden pommel and cantle of the age of armoured warfare was no more seen, even on the battlefield. Martingales were not in use but breast plates (petrels) and cruppers which were more like breechings than modern cruppers were common adjuncts of the riding saddle, as in medieval times.

Mounted groom leading horse in hand. This shows a conservative style of saddle more reminiscent of the war saddle of feudal times than of the *selle royale* of the late Renaissance. Woodcut from Fugger, *Von der Gestüterey*, 1584. (Reproduced by permission of Miland Publishers, Nieuwkoop, Netherlands)

Side-saddles had been in use for the past 200 years, and design had improved to some extent during that time, but they still had no stirrups and the rider's feet (or at any rate the right foot) rested on a planchette like a step. What is described as an 'Irish' side-saddle, the head chased and gilt, and the seat inlaid with down, was bought by the Cecils for £7 in 1610. Pillions for ladies' use also had planchettes, and were also known as cushions or pads. An item less familiar in the modern stable was the 'horse-lock' or 'fetter', a kind of thief-proof hobble not unlike handcuffs. They cost 3s 4d a set in 1595.

Otherwise the equipment for the riding horse was very similar to that in use today, except that stirrups and bits were made of brass and not yet nickelled over.

Sidesaddle with footcloth. Woodcut from Fugger, *Von der Gestüterey*, 1584. (Reproduced by permission of Miland Publishers, Nieuwkoop, Netherlands)

Spurs were often brass; the rowels, however, were of steel. Though bits, both snaffle and curb, were of the most varied design, they were only used with one rein, and the 'double bridle' incorporating bit and bridoon was unknown.

Clothing

As in all ages before that of Queen Victoria, the horseman suffered from the absence of any sort of waterproof clothing. The best he could do was to rely on leather, and also woollens of the thickest yarn and tightest weave. There were few items of male dress intended solely for use on horseback – no characteristic riding headgear, for instance. The one exception was boots. These were of thigh length for riding, though not always worn pulled up to their highest extent. They were not polished (indeed, few leather objects were polished at all). But they were meant to be kept clean, which was no mean chore in view of the acreage of leather involved. They were about the size of modern fishing waders, and a man was paid 1s at Hatfield in 1607 for 'making clean my Lord's boots'. This compares with another casual tip recorded in the same petty cash account which only amounted to 6d for skinning a dead horse. Boots and cloak together were all that might signify a man was about to ride off on a long journey, that and the 'riding rod' in his hand, sometimes called a yard because that was what it measured. It was commonly held upright when not in use. Only postmen used whips on horseback to comply with the injunction 'Haste, post, haste'.

Women's riding costume was more specialised. After 1600 it was often crowned by a broad-brimmed hat like a man's, turned down in front. Earlier, the Queen on horseback had favoured a round-crowned hat with narrow brim, and fashion as usual followed her lead. The main parts of the riding-habit, below the waist, did not differ essentially from the 'foot-mantel' worn by Chaucer's more genteel female pilgrims. What was missing was anything approaching the 'hoses' worn by the Wife of Bath. The riding-skirt was so voluminous that it was hoped its folds would muffle the rider's feet and protect them from the mud which was an inseparable complement to a journey on horseback. This purpose was also meant to be aided by the footcloth, an item of saddlery nowadays unknown, mentioned here along with clothing because its purpose was not to control or to protect the horse, but to shield the rider. It was like a saddle-cloth that hung down behind the stirrups (in the case of the side-saddle, behind the planchette) and was intended to stop the mud splashing up against the rider's leg.

❧ ❧ ❧

'Or wilt thou ride?' they ask Christopher Sly the tinker in the Induction to *The Taming of the Shrew*:

> Thy horses shall be trapp'd,
> Their harness studded all with gold and pearl.   (Induc., ii, 42–3)

The tinker with the hangover may think he is dreaming, but it is a *possible* dream. There really were ceremonial caparisons in which gold wire and gold leaf and at any rate semi-precious stones were used. The collective noun then in use for saddlery was 'furniture', as in *All's Well* (II, iii, 59): 'I'd give Bay Curtal and his furniture.' We saw above furniture coming to about £50 per horse. Now let us hear Bion, in *The Taming of the Shrew*, describing a set worth perhaps 10s all told, second hand, well suited to the parcel of cat's meat which it 'furnishes':

> … an old mothy saddle and stirrups of no kindred … with a half-cheeked bit and a
> headstall of sheep's leather, which, being restrained to keep him from stumbling,

hath been often burst and new-repaired with knots; one girth six times pieced, and a woman's crupper of velure, which hath two letters for her name fairly set down in studs, and here and there pieced with pack-thread.   (III, ii, 47, 54–61)

Repairing a crupper of this sort could cost sixpence, as Dromio of Ephesus tells us in *The Comedy of Errors* (I, ii, 55–6).

Characters as diverse as Petruchio, John of Gaunt, the Duke of York and Henry VI call for their riding boots or want them 'plucked' off, and complain because it hurts (as it still does). Riding-robes are worn by Lady Faulconbridge in *King John*, and as things worked out in the theatre this would be the identical outfit provided for Imogen in *Cymbeline*, a riding-suit suitable for a franklin's wife. There is a foot-cloth in *Richard III* (III, iv, 84) and spurs are everywhere. The legs of Young Faulconbridge in *King John* are compared with riding-rods (I, i, 140), but the only whip is found in the hand of Queen Mab's 'waggoner'.

11

The law

A high proportion of the laws which Shallow and Silence in *II Henry IV* would have had to administer in real life concerned, directly or indirectly, horses. To take the statute book literally, one gets the impression that Elizabethan England was as rigorously ruled in this matter as Frederician Prussia. But there was a wide gulf between theory and practice, because it would simply have been beyond the power of such as Dogberry and Verges in *Much Ado* to charge and present before a court any but a small proportion of offenders under the numerous Acts.

The roads on which horses travelled were maintained (if that is the word) under the terms of the Highways Act of 1555. Before that, upkeep of roads had been the responsibility of manor courts. But the manorial system had been in decay for a long time; it was almost in ruins already in the reign of the Queen's grandfather. Greater social mobility and the change-over to a cash economy had meant that the rights and duties of Lords of the Manor changed with ever greater frequency from one owner to the next. After the Dissolution of the Monasteries chaos was made worse by the transfer of responsibility from monastic houses which had nearly all held the lordship of at least one manor to lay holders, coupled sometimes with partition or amalgamations of existing units. By their Act, Philip and Mary had charged the parishes with the duty of road-mending, so that the waywardern became an officer of the parish instead of the manorial court leet. But this did not make the office any more welcome or easier to discharge (see Chapter 6 above). The Lord of a Manor could always command transport for road work from his tenants, and their labour. But a parish as such owned no horses (though some of them had carts and sleds) and could less easily command the personal service of parishioners than a landlord could that of his tenants. This is one of the reasons why the sixteenth century saw the lowest point to which the condition of English roads ever descended.

Sale of horses was strictly regulated. It is questionable whether sale by private treaty was legitimate at all, though it was common enough. All such sales and purchases must be in 'market overt' where they came under the terms of the Sale of Horses Act, also of 1555. Thereby change of ownership, with details of the price given, names of witnesses to the deal, and details identifying the horse, had to be entered in a Toll Book by the keeper of the market. Should the purchaser prove to be a Scot, the vendor would be liable to a fine of £40 under 32 Hen. VIII, plus a year's imprisonment under an Elizabethan Act of 1559.

Suppose one just *found* a horse? That would not be difficult, with so many unfenced roads and fields, and the general poverty of grazing which would tempt 'lane-creepers' to wander where the grass was greener. The finder of a stray on his own property was entitled to impound it, but it is doubtful whether he was entitled to work it while impounded, under the Act of 1555; he was obliged to keep and feed it for a year and a day before he could claim it for his own. And any time up to day 366 the owner might turn up to take home his property, fat if not fit.

The Act concerning 'market overt' regulated not only cash deals but exchanges, as is proved by the few surviving market books, as well as complicated bargains in which one party gives the other a dun trotting gelding in exchange for two yearling fillies and 14s to boot, handing back sixpence as 'luck money', and so on.

There were ways of acquiring a horse cheaply by means of the law: in cases where horses were being kept contrary to various statutes the private citizen who denounced or for that matter arrested the transgressor was entitled to half the value of the horse, which was confiscated, while the other half went to the Crown. Thus if a horse worth £30 were concerned one had the option either of taking £15 from the authorities or buying the horse for £15. This happened quite often in the Northern counties, where some dealer, knowingly or not, had sold a horse to a Scot whom some law-abiding citizen later intercepted and apprehended 'leading a horse toward the borders of Scotland'. (But we shall see below that a legalistic approach to questions of horseflesh was exceptional in counties north of the Tees at that time.) Another such source of cheap supply was recusants, or persons ill-advised enough not to frequent the same place of worship as that of the religious majority. Various laws forbade them to own horses above the value of £2 or so (this varied from time to time), and if a justice could be found to assess the value of a recusant's horse anyone might buy it from him, if it were found to be worth more, for that sum.

One could of course breed one's own horses; but it was the breeder who had, ever since the early years of Henry VIII's reign, been most subject to government control, at any rate on paper. Down to the Reformation there had been, broadly speaking, four traditional ways of breeding horses. The most widespread, practised not only by substantial farmers but, in certain areas, by the meanest of labourers who held a toft and a croft and grazing rights on the common, resembled that practised in parts of Wales and on Dartmoor today. This consisted of turning out mares on the common grazing, often very extensive but always very poor, to be covered by whatever stallion or uncut colt happened to 'haunt' (as they still say in the New Forest) that stretch of heath or mountain or fen. At an annual 'drift' of the common, large or small, owners combined to round up their mares and youngstock, to brand the foals of that year (or earmark them) and to take off those old enough to sell at the autumn fairs or break for work. Originally the Lords of Manors had had mares and their followers running on these grazings along with those of humbler folk, but by the late sixteenth century this was an exceptional state of affairs. Up to 1539 monastic houses had been among the Lords of Manors, and these, but especially the Cistercian houses, had taken part in this 'rough' breeding, as names of mountain pasture such as Abbotside and Fountains Fell in the Pennines still testify. But the great Cistercian houses were the pioneers of English stock improvement, and by their more rigorous policy of castrating unsuitable colts and keeping mares in enclosures with selected stallions until they were safely in foal and might be turned out on the fell, they had done much to raise local standards; notably in the North, where the 'tried breed of the North Country' was acknowledged to be that kept by the brothers of Jervaulx in Wensleydale.

Besides this 'mountain and moorland' system and its improved version as practised by the monks, which between them produced only farm horses and pack horses (mostly very small) with some general-purpose riding-horses and a select grade of palfreys almost exclusively of monastic breeding, there was breeding by the landowning class on a system which became more widespread at about the time of the Dissolution of the Monasteries. It became rarer and rarer during the reigns of the first two Tudor monarchs for landowners to rely, for large game, on an extensive 'chase' comprising almost the whole uncultivated part of their estates. Instead they would enclose or 'empale' part of it, and stock it with fallow or roe deer and hares. In this deer-park they would also run brood mares, secure from the unwelcome attentions of the tenants' colts. These mares were intended to produce riding horses for travel and for hunting, of the type described by Blundeville as 'fair ambling horses to travel by the waie'.

There still remained some remnant of a fourth system, a variation on the deer-park stud, practised only by the Crown and originally administered by the Constables of royal castles all over the country. Every such castle had a park in which grazed, all the year round, a stud of 'great' mares from which war horses were bred. These mares never left the park where they had been foaled, but in the breeding season there were turned out with them two stallions of the same stamp which rotated periodically to avoid in-breeding, and so might be drawn from any part of the country. Thus we know from the scant surviving records that stallions from Merton in Surrey and Tutbury in Staffordshire had been assigned to cover mares at Pickering in Yorkshire in 1326. The system seems to have been devised by Edward I, and had its headquarters at Windsor. By about 1580 all that was left of it was at Windsor, at Hampton Court, at Tutbury and at Malmesbury; and even there the breeding programme was changing over from heavyweight chargers to 'running horses'.

Henry VIII had not been devoid of military ambition, by fits and starts, and at one time was determined to maintain land forces that would match those in the pay of the Emperor or the King of France. But he shrank from the expense of mounting the cavalry arm, and determined that this cost should be borne, and the attendant trouble and risks taken, by his subjects according to their degree. His laws to this end were in force down to 1603 and later. As we saw in Chapter 3, the stallions were now to be kept by peers and higher ecclesiastics, though not by knights and gentlemen as such, but by persons with a cash income of £100 and above. The scale ranged from eight stallions for an archbishop or a duke down to one for a person with £100 a year or a wife who habitually wore clothes of a quality specified in the Act, passed in the thirty-eighth year of his reign, which came into effect in 1545.

The mares and the way they were kept were a rationalisation of the third system described above. By an Act of 1536 all owners of deer-parks had to keep brood mares in them, capable of bearing foals 'apt for service in the wars', the intention being that they should be served by stallions kept under the provisions of the Act mentioned in the last paragraph. Deer-parks with a perimeter of one mile had to maintain two such brood mares, those with a four-mile pale four mares, and so in proportion, according to the extent of ground empaled.

As to the first or 'mountain and moorland' system, the decline in the standard of horses (or ponies) kept on common grazings was a direct result, according to Catholic historians, of the Dissolution of the Monasteries, and according to Protestant historians of the fact that the monastic standards of husbandry had been going steadily downhill for years before 1539. An infidel historian might take the view that 'rough' grazing of this kind was being pressed beyond its true capabilities by the greatly increased stocking with sheep, which are more formidable competitors with horses for grazing than if cattle and horses are run on the same hill, and that the market for horses of the stamp in which the great monastic houses had specialised was rather slow, owing to the increased demand for trotting horses to ride.

But from highest to lowest it was the breeder on extensive grazing all over the country who was the target for the great volley of Tudor legislation. Specifications of minimum height for stallions turned out on commons were laid down (and altered) in successive Acts, and there were directions for culling at the annual 'drifts' of those youngstock not 'able or like to grow to profitable labours' in the judgement of – of all people – the owners! Here again there was much reliance on stool-pigeons. An informant might, after denouncing the owner to the justices, take possession of a sub-standard stallion depastured on common grazing as his reward, and there was absolutely nothing to prevent his breeding from it, either on some other common until denounced in his turn or on his own enclosed ground.

Even the price of feeding-stuffs was controlled, a scale of prices being periodically fixed. One such, drawn up in 1588, prices oats at 13d a bushel and beans or pease (also classed as 'Horsemeate') at 12s a quarter. The standard loaf of horsebread, enough for one feed for one full-sized horse, was controlled at a halfpenny, and by-laws of some boroughs forbade 'brownbakers' who made the stuff to bake bread for human consumption on the same premises. Yet it was notoriously impossible to define at what point the better sort of horsebread shaded off into the coarser sort of man-bread – what the German Army used to call *Komissbrot*.

Export of horses was not so much controlled as forbidden. It was a felony to 'carry out of the realm beyond sea any horse or gelding or any mare' above the value of 6s 8d. Even then, you could not get much of a mare for 6s 8d, anywhere. Horses for one's own use might be shipped abroad under special licence, but if they did not come back with their owner the immigration officer would want to know the reason why.

The justification for most of these laws was national security, one way and another, and there was nothing new about them. For instance, the ban on exports can be matched with earlier laws from the reign of King Athelstan, 600 years and thirty-four reigns before Elizabeth. Those who see in such laws a tribute to the superiority of English horses should reflect that every kingdom in Christendom, and some outside it, had at one time or another similar laws. So long as horses were in some sort munitions of war, the law aimed to deny them to those sinister but not permanently identifiable characters, the Queen's enemies.

Similarly, the laws concerning breeding were framed primarily with a view to maintaining the supply of remounts; not only for the permanent forces which were very small and now included only a small element of heavy cavalry (hence the run-down of the royal establishment for breeding chargers), but for the horsed contingent of the county militias – the 'powers of the shires'. Here theoretically out of every ten pressed men one ought to be mounted, but as a light-horseman or 'demi-lance', not as a man-at-arms. It was for this reason that the stallions turned out on the commons were not to be smaller than fourteen (in some cases thirteen) hands high. For reasons explained in Chapter 14 below, the law required the stallions kept by peers and richer citizens to trot.

In this latter respect official breeding policy as expressed in the legal code did not make sense in the light of practical experience or of the written works on horse-breeding that have come down to us from that age. Breeders agreed that a pacing mare would throw pacing foals, most of the time, to any stallion, even a 'great stoned trotting horse'; while a trotting mare, if covered by a pacing stallion, would be more likely than not to produce a trotting foal. But the specification for the mares to be kept in deer-parks was purely one of height; the law did not lay down that they should trot.

This is only one aspect of the unrealistic nature of these laws, which is thrown into relief by the frequency with which they were re-enacted, each time in a more stringent form. Elizabethan governments tried to reinforce them by screwing up the penalties a little higher each time: heavier fines, imprisonment, confiscation, corporal punishment including hanging for horse-theft. Of positive encouragement to breeders there is no trace – always the stick, never the carrot. The laws remained unenforceable to the end, because in spite of inducements offered to common informers, the machinery for detecting and punishing infringement was so inadequate.

Bargain and sale
Market prices of agricultural horses varied more, from county to county, than the price of saddle horses, the various categories of which were equally in demand in all parts of the country, and to which more or less uniform standards of value applied, according to quality. With agricultural horses the case was different, largely owing to the patchy development of arable technique. Some shires were still working arable holdings entirely on the Anglo-Saxon system of ox-ploughing, four or six or eight oxen to the team. In others, such as East Anglia and large areas of the North Country, horse ploughing was already general. In such areas, a team of two horses to go in the plough commanded a respectable price, about what one would pay for six oxen, or three 'yokes', of differing ages, between two and seven years old. In most of the shires adjacent to London ox-ploughing was still general and the husbandmen only used their horses for carting and to carry packloads. Always bearing in mind that executors' valuations were on the careful side, somewhat below the day's market price, inventories of Kentish wills (from the

ox-plough zone) are significant. Thus the stock of Robert Baldock of Charing as of 19 June 1567 included one yoke of three-year-old oxen and one yoke of four-year-old oxen worth £6 (9 marks) the lot, or £1 10s apiece. His cows were worth £1 each. But his five horses consisting of one mare, one gelding and three youngsters of one, two and three years old were only worth £6 the lot, or 24s a head. In the North Country at this time agricultural mares fetched a minimum of £2 a head, and geldings rather more, if sound. The inventory to the will of Thomas Foster of Cranbrook, in October 1584, shows an even lower horse price relative to that of working oxen. His oxen were valued at £2 each, near the value of an East Anglian or North Country plough horse; but Cranbrook is in the Weald, on heavy clay. Oxen were good for working this sort of ground, but it required very strong oxen. His two mares and three colts together were written down at £3 10s: probably £1 each for the mares and half that for the colts. Even the horses belonging to a very substantial yeoman of this county, Symon Autreys of Norton, whose farm contained fifty acres of arable besides pasture, were only valued at £21 for eight fully grown animals, one of which was for riding, and so might well have been valued at £5, making the rest only around £2 5s 8d each. This was also in 1567.

One rung up the social scale in the same county shows only a slight difference in the price (quality) of horses owned. John Toke, Gent, of Great Chart, died in 1565 possessed of two 'nagges' (riding horses) worth only £2 each, two 'ould geldings' at £1 each, a grey mare, £2 13s 4d, a 'sorrell yong mare', £2, her foal, 6s 8d, besides a mare worth £2 10s, and two colts and a filly worth £3 the lot, running on Romney Marsh. The most expensive horses he owned were two young geldings at £4 10s each, also running on the Marsh. These would be the esteemed (and costly) Scottish trotting geldings, put out on the rich marsh grazing to recover from their long march down from the Border.

☙ ☙ ☙

The law relating to horses is almost a blank in Shakespeare's works, as is crime (see Chapter 12), and indeed it would be very odd if one figured to any extent without the other in the plays. But then, lawyers and legal matters in general do not bulk large in them. So far as the comedy side is concerned, the author probably estimated that the majority of his audience could not possibly see anything funny in the law, so left it alone. And having created so bright and attractive a heroine as Portia, he chose the legal disguise as one dull enough to enhance these qualities by contrast.

Of all the manifold ways in which the law might impinge on the horseman, as outlined summarily above, it only affects Falstaff when, in *The Merry Wives of*

Windsor, he pledges his horses to mine host of The Garter, whose patience in the last act is exhausted to the point of foreclosure. Probably the knight has not paid for them in the first place, when Bardolph had 'gone into Smithfield to buy your worship a horse' (*II Henry IV* I, ii, 50). But if it came to a liquidation, they were Sir John's obvious tangible asset.

12

Crime

Surprisingly, among the more disreputable persons of Shakespeare's dramas there is no professional horse-thief, and little reference in his plays to this widespread and lucrative criminal activity. Even the slang used in some of the more baffling prose dialogue contains no element, not a single word, of the special thieves' cant used in the daily traffic of horse stealing.

This was a huge business, entailing large capital investment and heavy current expenses, for there were outgoings all the time, in the form of bribes, rent of stabling, forage and fodder. It was not worth a thief's while to under-feed a stolen horse; if he did not sell it in as good or better condition than it was in when he 'prigged' it, the operation would not be worth the risks attending a capital felony.

The elaborate rules for market procedure laid down in the Sale of Horses Act, 1555, were all designed to make if not the theft then at least the disposal of stolen horses more difficult. And almost every provision of that Act gave employment to some classes of hanger-on of the horse-stealing interest to perform some useful service for the master-thief. For instance, there had to be witnesses to every transaction in market overt which was entered in the Toll Book; consequently every mart was haunted by out-of-work post-boys who for a small consideration would make their mark to a testimony that they had known buyer and seller for many years, and were well aware that the horse was the property of the vendor. There were innkeepers who must be paid to ask no questions, and farriers who without batting an eyelid must be persuaded to remove a perfectly good new set of shoes and replace them with possibly much worse fitting but obviously different ones, or to obliterate brands in the hoof, and perhaps burn in new ones. Sometimes locksmiths had to be paid to remove the 'fetters' or metal hobbles in which horses, specially on the outskirts of large towns, were turned out to graze. This illegal branch of the craft was known as the 'black-art', only one of the many expressions peculiar to the horse-thief which show, by the very amount of space they take up in Thomas Dekker's social satire, *The Gull's Hornbook* (1609), what a very large and important sector of the underworld it was that used this sub-dialect of thieves' cant; proportionally larger than the share of the car-thief in today's criminal economy. Another expensive item was the custom-made saddlery for criminal use, which called for special materials and fine workmanship: a treeless saddle, for instance, made entirely of quilting and so compactly that, with its girth, it would go into one 'hose-slop' (trouser pocket) while the special soft leather bridle and reins went into the other; folding spurs; riding-boots made of such fine leather that they could be carried in a lawyer's brief-bag without bulging more than would a book or a roll of parchment.

Like the motor-stealing business, the 'prancer-prigging lay' benefited greatly by the acute parking problem. With the steady increase in agricultural production, more and more people frequented the weekly markets. All buyers, and most sellers, came on horseback. The stables of all town inns were full to capacity on market days, and late-arriving market-goers might have to content themselves with tying their horses up in the inn-yard. Ostlers had enough to do with feeding and watering, and might be more concerned with collecting the right amount of bait money plus appropriate tip than with noting just who paid the reckoning and took the horse away. After dinner those customers who were not drunk had at least drink taken, so that reactions would be slow and clumsy, even if the cry of 'stop thief' were raised.

Another weekly occasion of great profit to the horse-thief was Sunday. Under the Elizabethan Settlement everybody had to go to church – the right church – weekly, and there were heavy fines for recusancy. In the more thickly populated shires, churches lay so close together that nearly everybody, questions of prestige apart, might walk to church. But there were, especially in the North and West, some vast and sparsely peopled parishes like Williton in Somerset or Chester-le Street in Durham or Romaldkirk in Yorkshire, where people whose home was near the parish boundary might have half a day's journey to church and home again. Nobody would choose to do this on foot, if they had the means to ride. Not all churches were actually in villages, and where they stood in open country there was commonly an inn, the property of the church, close by, but the pressure on its stabling would be greater than that of the urban inns on market day. There were two alternatives if there was no stall at the inn: either to turn the horse out, if possible hobbled, in some 'horse-close' next to the churchyard, or to get someone who was not legally obliged to be in church to 'walk' the horse in hand until the rider came out. This was only one of the occasions on which even a prudent man like Master Ford of Windsor must, sooner or later, 'trust … a thief to walk my ambling gelding' (*Merry Wives of Windsor* II, ii, 293).

There was also a class of cheat, rather than thief, who frequented inn stables. You might call him a bent horse-doctor. He had enough veterinary knowledge to produce temporarily the symptoms of acute colic in a likely looking horse. When the distraught owner had been summoned he would offer to practise his infallible cure, but only on condition that no one else should see him at work, on the pretext of not wishing to divulge the priceless secret of his art. Once alone, he would work his miraculous cure by simply undoing his own work. Or else he would offer to buy the horse as it stood, for a knock-down price.

Although the sort of stealing described above was the work of highly organised gangs with a widespread network, which in the course of a year made away with a great number of horses, these were stolen singly or in twos and threes, only those of high value being selected. Whenever possible the act was carried out without violence, not because this would lessen the penalty of a convicted thief, but because of the risk of damaging the horse, and because the 'priggers' and their backers the 'lancemen' do not seem to have been violent types and had few connections with the rest of the underworld.

But another kind of robbery brought a great many 'hot' (to use a modern item of thieves' cant) horses into the market, the lifting of which might well have cost lives. Along the borders of Scotland there were still some communities, such as that of Kirk Yetholm and sundry places in Redesdale, whose profession was robbery, chiefly of livestock. The rustling took place mainly on the other side of the border, and the booty was sold in English markets; but some was stolen in England by such as the 'robars of Reidisdale' and the zone of such operations extended much further south than is commonly supposed. A ballad called 'Rookhope Ride' was still being sung in Weardale, County Durham, in the 1780s, which recounts, with much circumstantial detail, a foray undertaken by certain men of the Bampton district against Stanhope in County Durham, taking advantage of the disturbed conditions occasioned by the Rising of the North, to steal sheep and horses in 1569. This raid did not come off, but had it done so, the booty would eventually have been sold by means of agents or 'marters' who more commonly acted for the peaceful 'lancemen', in South-country markets. But first the animals would have been thoroughly disguised – brands altered, shoes changed, hair dyed, manes shorn, ears nicked and so on. Between these two extremes of larceny and fraud on the one hand and what amounted to private warfare on the other, every variation on the horse-stealing theme was practised every day.

The methods by which horses were disguised on the orders of thieves or

receivers were a close secret among corrupt farriers. Even those who were 'scholars' would be reluctant to commit the secrets of the art to writing, and we have
little detailed knowledge of how these transformations were effected. By pure
accident, two of their recipes found their way into print as veterinary notes
appended to a work on horsemanship by that eminently respectable gentleman of
Kent, some time of the Inns of Court. It was vital for the mounted rustler operating
by night that his horse should be as silent as the rider; he must therefore know how

To Make a Horse that he shall not Neigh
Tie a woolen list about the midest of his tonge, and he shall not ney so long as it
remaineth.

As for disguise, or as an aid in selling a horse of the notoriously unlucky all-black
colour, what more useful than the recipe

To Make a White Mark on a Black Horse
Take a Tile and burn it to powder; take derris roots, and the roots of white bryer, of
each a like, dry them, make powder thereof, then shave the place that you will have
white, rub it very much with the powder, then wash the place with this water: take a
quantity of honeysuckle flowers, and a quantity of honey, and the water that Moles
have been sodden in, and wash the place, and rub it very sore therewith: doe this five
daies, and keep him from all winds, and it will be white.

Glendower, Douglas and the Percies junior and senior had, of course, all stolen
horses in their time. It was part of the frontier life-style. So in *II Henry IV* when
Old Northumberland is seeking intelligence of his son's progress in his southern
adventure, and somebody dismisses bad news as an invention of the (off-stage)
informant, a bad character 'that had stol'n the horse he rode on' (I, i, 57), we may
assume the tongue is in the cheek. Apart from these very superior rustlers, we have
only the mysterious 'Germans' of *The Merry Wives* who stole the Slough postmaster's horses by fraud. Otherwise we have only a negative mention, in *As You
Like It*, when Celia says: 'Yes, I think he is not a pick-purse nor a horse-stealer' (II,
iv, 21).

13

Hunting and falconry

HUNTING

Officially, we count the end of the Middle Ages from the day Queen Elizabeth's grandfather Henry VII came to the throne, and if the transitions between medieval and modern cannot be measured very evenly in all spheres of human activity in England, at least in the matter of hunting, and the balance of man against nature, it works out very typically according to the standard pattern. 'Defensive' hunting in many parts of the realm was still a reality in 1485, the year of the Battle of Bosworth Field: that is, there was a situation still in which men had to hunt certain animals because otherwise their living would be destroyed by the wild game ravaging the crops or beasts of prey decimating the flocks. Settled, regularly farmed country in medieval England was a group of islands in a sea of waste lands. Whereas in the England of Elizabeth there was a sea of settled land, and the wilderness had been reduced to an ever-shrinking archipelago within it.

This meant that the variety of hunting available in England was much narrower in Shakespeare's lifetime than it had been in the reign of Henry VII. Local traditions about the death of 'the last wolf in England' mostly refer to the reign of that king (whereas in Wales they relate to the reign of James I). The English habitat of the wild boar was dwindling fast. Red deer were becoming very scarce south of the Trent. Roe were patchily distributed, perhaps not much more common than they are now, except in the North Country. Fallow deer were found everywhere, artificially preserved in empaled parks, and there was a great deal of re-stocking from one park to another, often over long distances.

There is some evidence to show that the English wolf did not quite die out before the accession of Henry VIII, but certainly it did not survive the Reformation by more than a year or two.* Folk memory of its baneful presence was still vivid, and it would seem that Shakespeare knew plenty of old men (not necessarily Welshmen) who had seen a live wolf in their youth. The last English person to be eaten by a wild wolf was a baby snatched from its cradle near Kington, Herefordshire, in James I's reign. The wolf almost certainly had its den on Fforest Fawr in Wales. The wild cat was still fairly plentiful, though no one any longer kept a pack of hounds exclusively for the chase of this game.

In general, hunting meant in practice the pursuit of the hare in open country and of the fallow deer in parks and chases. The old distinctions between forests (exclusively royal, so far as hunting went), chases, parks and warrens were becoming blurred. Forest law still existed, on paper, but was little observed in practice, at least in all the minute ramifications noted by such writers as John Manwood, whose interest was as much antiquarian as practical. There were still many royal forests, but increasingly the court was ceasing to progress through the realm; it was becoming sedentary in the Southeast, and it was a long time since the monarch had hunted in any forest north of Sherwood or west of Shotover. People were still being 'presented' (prosecuted) in courts of swainmoot for such old-fashioned offences as killing game in the purlieus or immediate surroundings of forests, but the whole question was being taken less and less seriously. In terms of game laws, England was in the middle of a mild spell, midway between the savage penal sanctions of late Norman times, in which a 'foreign' aristocracy and royal house were asserting their exclusive rights of venery by means of corporal punishment, and the Georgian period when game was much scarcer and the squirearchy was protecting its share of what was left by means of fines, imprisonment and transportation. For some centuries before Elizabeth's accession the law had been fighting a losing battle against the poacher over a wide social spectrum. The respectable social status of persons appearing before the special forest courts is remarkable throughout the period. Thus in the fourteenth century, at one session of Pickering Forest Court in Yorkshire, not only was a villein (no doubt the forefather of some deadly Yorkshire fast bowlers) presented for taking a red stag by throwing stones at it, but also three armigeral gentlemen had stood trial for taking deer in the forest and setting up a stag's head on a stake in insulting contempt of the Duke of Lancaster's forester. At the end of the sixteenth century, persons presented in forest courts for poaching and for armed affray with keepers frequently included persons in holy orders, undergraduates and even dons of

---

* It is fairly certain from the evidence of parish registers not now extant that the last English wolves were killed in the Vale (then a marsh) of Pickering, North Yorkshire, in 1540–5. The killers received scalp bounty from public funds.

universities. Thus if the story about Shakespeare's taking deer from Sir Thomas Lucy's park as a young man is true, this was not, in the context of the time, a particularly 'low-class' offence. Nor was it a particularly rural one. Townspeople lived very close to the country in every sense, though only the citizens of London had their own forest (Epping), just like the monarch. That very urban comedy, Thomas Dekker's *Shoemaker's Holiday* (1600), has a racy account of the illegal taking of deer in the purlieus of Epping.

Foxhunting, contrary to a belief widespread today, did exist in the England of William Shakespeare, but it was relatively unimportant; also unspecialised, and did not always take place on horseback. It was similar to the pursuit of the otter and the still frequent polecat and marten, more a form of vermin control; no landowner had a proprietary interest in these small carnivores in the sense of game preservation. The same was true of the wild cat and its hunting, which was done on horseback in those counties, including the whole of Wales and much of the North Country, where it was still found.

As to the hare, there was coursing with greyhounds, then as now a mixture of hunting and dog-racing, on moorland and downland and on the Wolds of Lincolnshire and East Yorkshire. For hare-hunting proper, a different stamp of hound was employed, slower than the modern foxhound and somewhat smaller, hunting exclusively by scent and selected among other qualities for the timbre of its voice. The Elizabethan hare-hunter laid enormous stress on the 'music' of hounds in full cry, and to have a pack that gave tongue in harmony was just as important as to have one that killed a lot of hares.

In the hunting of the deer at least two kinds of hound were used in every establishment, tufters or lymers which set the game on foot, and the running hounds which pursued buck or hart until it stood to bay. The same was true of what was left of boar-hunting.

Although in theory red-deer hunting took precedence over all other forms of venery, in practice the hunting of the boar was more prized by those who could get it. It was the last wild animal left in England that was dangerous to man, and in the lifetime of Shakespeare it was already extinct in the South Country. The Queen's late father, when he was courting Jane Seymour, had hunted the boar on the Wolfhall estate of the Seymours in Wiltshire. But there is some evidence which implies that the game was not bred at Wolfhall, and that already at that date it had been necessary to obtain it from some quite different source, and 'turn it down' for the occasion. James I was ready to hunt anything that would run, any day of the week, but the only record of his having hunted wild boar was in an account of his entertainment at Whalley in Lancashire, and by that time boar had become very scarce even in the Cumbrian region. Where they did linger, contrary to the usual pattern of survival and extinction in England whereby the last representatives of a wild species are found either in the far North or the far West, was in the wooded parts of the Midlands. The last English wild boar lived and died on Cannock Chase in Staffordshire in Charles II's time, and there were still some in Shakespeare's Warwickshire. They seem to have been jealously preserved and artificially fed in winter, for the allusion to Falstaff in *II Henry IV* (II, ii, 138) about the old boar feeding in 'the old frank' mentions the special pens where keepers put out food for the wild swine in hard weather.

A boy brought up in the West Midlands would be able to recognise, and to associate with living realities, any reference to the boar hunt encountered in classical literature; and if he treated the subject in imitation of the ancients he would still be able to describe such a hunt not in terms copied from his source but according to the native conventions of the boar hunt now becoming somewhat rare but familiar enough in his father's day. Whereas a Londoner born and bred could never have come across a wild boar even two days' (normal) journey from home. All that was left of the creature, for him, were the inn signs over the doors of such hostelries as the famous one in Eastcheap. The Greeks and the Romans hunted the boar on foot, but when Shakespeare tackles the subject, in *Venus and Adonis*, he mounts the boar-hunter, who will not dismount until the quarry turns at bay. This was the English convention of the time, in real life.

Shakespeare's description of the game is striking, and unrivalled in any quarter. Granted that it is put into the mouth of Venus, and that the whole passage is meant to frighten and deter Adonis from his object, her description (line 618) of the boar as 'a mortal butcher, bent to kill' is realistic enough.

At the end of the poem several hounds are seen dying of the boar's attack, and the execution which he did to horses, hounds and men was notorious. For this reason alone boar-hunting in sixteenth-century England, now that there were no more wolves, deserved the epithet 'image of war'. It was an accepted maxim that although the roles of some breeds of hound were interchangeable, as between hare and roe hunting, for instance, you could not 'force' the boar with any hounds but the powerful mastiff-like sort that were bred for this game alone. The after-effects of a 'stroke' from the boar's tushes could be horrible. For they were not only weapons, they were also tools with which he rooted for underground food:

> His snout digs sepulchres ... (622)

and thus more often than not they were charged with the earth-borne bacilli of tetanus, so that a mere scratch from them would cause the victim to come down with the dreaded lockjaw, for which no remedy was known.

The wedge-like build of the boar, and his 'brawny sides with hairy bristles armed' (625), enabled him to charge through dense thickets of briar, bramble and blackthorn which would close after him, impenetrable to horse and hound alike, and unless he were attacked from a certain angle at points which he took care not to expose, his hide was 'better proof than thy spear's point can enter' (626).

This is like a distant echo of the boar hunt in Lancashire described two centuries earlier in *Gawain and the Green Knight*:

> But the poyntes pared at the pyth that pyght in his scheldes ...

> *But the points [of arrows] were turned that hit his flanks.*   (1456)

At that time a boar's flanks were actually called 'shields'. The sheer terror inspired by the aspect of the boar has never been made more comprehensible than by its masterly description in *Venus and Adonis*, lines 619–24.

The ideal boar-hunting horse, therefore, must partake to some extent of the nature of a warhorse. It would be required – though the occasion would not be sought by the rider, who at the 'moment of truth' would attack on foot – to withstand an unexpected charge by the quarry bursting from his ambush. 'Courage' in the normal horseman's sense of the willingness to go on galloping or to go on jumping beyond the limit of endurance of other animals would not be enough. The boar-hunter's horse must understand, and not be averse to, infighting if need be. It is not surprising, then, that Adonis rides a stallion.

Whatever the game might be, however, the most striking difference between then and now is the fact that in the Elizabethan hunting field the great majority of horses ridden were stallions. That is not to say that entire horses are utter strangers to this activity at the present day: they are, perhaps, increasingly seen. But broadly speaking this is the exception – the typical modern hunter is a gelding. Embarrassing incidents of the kind that happened in *Venus and Adonis* are more likely to occur in the autumn and the early spring, at the beginning and end of the hunting season. But even so, those who ride stallions to hounds are ever ready to point out (to all hearers) that while being ridden the horse never thinks about anything *but* being ridden. But then, Adonis' hunter did not tear loose from the ragged bough while Adonis was on board. What happens when the stallion comes unridden? Under today's conditions he would make straight for the most attractive mare present, and one may reckon that perhaps a quarter of the hunters out on any given day are, in our times, mares. When Shakespeare was writing the result would be more likely to be a fight between the loose stallion and one of the others, without any very serious consequences, since stallions do little more than spar at each other unless stimulated by the presence of a mare actually on heat. This presence would be highly unusual in an Elizabethan context. In the section 'Of Hunting Horses' in his *Historie of Foure-Footed Beastes* (1607), Edward Topsell says:

> The males are much better than the females, and therefore they seldom use mares in hunting, because they are not so well able to leape, or endure the woodes ...

Of these two, enduring the woods was far more important, especially after boar. Indeed, at that time one would be far more likely to incur the Master's displeasure by appearing mounted on a mare than by anything else. And if you came out on a 'horsing' mare he would be liable to strike you dead!

PARK HUNTING

A great deal of buck-hunting took place in parks, mentioned above in the context of horse-breeding. Throughout the quarter-century of our study, there was a continuous increase in 'empalement' of parks, of which 700 were marked on Christopher Saxton's *Atlas of England* (1575). There were at least a thousand by the end of the sixteenth century. By 1617 Fynes Moryson could say 'Every gentleman of £500 and £1000 rent by the year hath a park inclosed with payles of wood for two or three myles compass.' And he reckoned, certainly wrongly, that there were more fallow deer in one English county than in the rest of Europe beside. Some gentlemen made parks on land which did not entirely belong to them, but on which the grazing rights – 'the herbage thereof' – was shared with other freeholders. The latter were not enraged by this encroachment on their rights. They still had the grazing inside the pale, and if they had been running the same stock on the open common, or even on their own land which they had not the capital to fence, they would have had to employ a herdboy. From time to time some Jeremiah would raise a loud lament on economic grounds, that land was being taken up by parks that otherwise could have been put to more profitable use. It is doubtful if this was really so. No landlord at that time would turn into a park land of any worthwhile arable potential – otherwise his rent-roll would soon cease to add up to £1000 or even £500. At best, land enclosed by pales was medium-quality pasture. It was not impossible to make hay in suitable tracts of a park. The little vignettes which embellish estate maps of the period commonly show cattle and sheep, besides horses, grazing in deer-parks.

Some such parks were subdivided internally, as the accompanying contem-

Plan of Windsor Park by John Norden, 1607. (The British Library, Harl. 3749 88–5v–5*).

porary engraving of Windsor Park, scene of Falstaff's appearance as Herne the Hunter (*Merry Wives of Windsor*), shows. Windsor, though the most famous of such parks, was by no means the biggest. The 'pale within a pale' on the north side of the Little Park towards Datchet Ferry was called 'The Course', and was typical of many such, long and narrow. Park hunting did not resemble any form of hunting now practised in England. On the one hand it was much more like hare coursing, and the purpose of 'The Course' was to test the prowess of individual hounds or to match one hound against another. On the other hand it came close to the form of hunting then practised in France and Spain, a battue in a confined space.

'The Standings' marked on this map was a sort of covered pavilion from which the royal party could practise archery against moving targets driven towards them

A view of Windsor looking across 'The Course' to the castle. Engraving by Hoefnagel. (Reproduced by courtesy of the Trustees of the British Museum)

by beaters. This scarcely required the use of horses except to get to the shooting point from the Castle, though of course coursing could hardly be followed on foot.

Another form of hunting requiring the use of horses was the business of keepers ('parkers') rather than their employers. This was stalking, done either to cull individual deer that were undesirable for breeding purposes, to control numbers, or simply to provide venison for the table of the great house, or as a gift, when my lord was not hunting. As cover, the shooter had recourse to a stalking horse, a custom that has its roots in the remote past and may well have been the earliest use of the horse, in so far as the species may have been domesticated by hunters as opposed to pastoralists. The practice survived in rare instances into the nineteenth century in England.* Since above all the stalking horse had to be steady, it was often old; often blind also, it is said. Park deer, like the wild deer of the forest, had no fear of horses as such, and the shooter got within range by keeping his horse between him and the target. Once there, he discharged his harquebus or caliver either over its withers or under its belly.

ꙮ ꙮ ꙮ

The third scene of Act III in *Macbeth* is laid at Forres, in 'a park, with a road leading to the palace'. Though this is Scotland in the Viking Age, it is quite clear that the dramatist visualised the setting as something exactly like what was to be encountered in the English Home Counties, *circa* 1606. The general layout of Forres 'palace' and its grounds must resemble Windsor Castle, on a rather more modest scale. The great house is set at one side of a deer-park, which like many such parks, including Windsor, is rather long and narrow. The three murderers lie in wait at dusk under the shadow of the deer-park palings. The third, whom many critics believe to be Macbeth himself, partly because of his familiarity with the layout of the grounds and the habits of the residents and guests at the great house, replies to the First Murderer's 'His horses go about' with:

> Almost a mile; but he does usually,
> So all men do, from hence to the palace gate
> Make it their walk.   (III, iii, 12)

What we have to envisage is a park of quite modest dimensions, more or less the standard two-mile compass, with probably only three gates capable of admitting horses or wheeled vehicles. Of these, one leads from the park to the forecourt in front of the 'palace'; as the Second Murderer says:

---

* The early-nineteenth-century animal painter, James Ward, painted a stalking horse.

<blockquote>
the rest
That are within the note of expectation,
Already are i' th' court.   (III, iii, 9)
</blockquote>

The ambush has been laid at a point in the pale directly opposite the court gate, and perhaps not more than 200 yards (a bowshot) distant from it across the middle of the park. The other two gates will be at the ends of the park, guarded by lodges in which the keepers and their families live. Drives lead from these lodges to the court gate, and persons making a ceremonial entry would not dream of using any other approach. But Banquo, Fleance and party have only been for an afternoon's ride in the country on the far side of the park from the house. At the point where the murderers lurk is one of several 'deer-leaps' through which a buck can pass into the park, but not out; which a man can negotiate either way round, but which is impassable to a horse, ridden, led or loose (since all such parks served also as paddocks for brood mares). The cloppety-clop, stamp-stamp in the wings is Banquo and Fleance dismounting, handing their horses to the groom to lead round outside the palings. The victims enter by climbing or squeezing through the deer-leap.

It is patent throughout the plays that hunting, not racing, is regarded as the sport of kings, and indeed since the time of King Alfred down to that day there had been no monarch who did not hunt regularly, and few who did not enjoy it. Many kings in very reduced circumstances still hunted, as, for instance, Alfred himself did during his dark days in Athelney.

So it is not surprising that among the many amenities offered to King Henry VI, when in the all-too-lenient protective custody of the Bishop of Ripon, was hunting; and his escape was not too hard to contrive from a deer-park at Middleham, near the junction of Coverdale and Wensleydale. Robert Morden's map of the North Riding shows no less than three deer-parks close to Middleham, besides Bishopdale Chase between Buckden Pike and Stake Moss, where red deer were still to be found in the seventeenth century.

The counterpart of the Dauphin, with his intemperate flow of horse-chat, is Theseus in *A Midsummer Night's Dream*, ably seconded by his 'bouncing Amazon' Hippolyta. How they do rattle on about their hounds and the noise they make, 'Slow in pursuit, but match'd in mouth like bells' (IV, i, 122).

The same desirable quality is found in the hounds offered to Tinker Sly in the Induction to *The Taming of the Shrew*:

<blockquote>
Or wilt thou hunt?
Thy hounds shall make the welkin answer them
And fetch shrill echoes from the hollow earth.   (Induc. ii, 45–7)
</blockquote>

It would be sufficiently obvious from this play alone that the object of hunting was not simply to gallop across country. If you were not prepared to take an interest in hound-work you might as well not go out. As the Lord says:

> Saw'st thou not, boy, how Silver made it good,
> At the hedge corner, in the coldest fault?   (Induc. i, 17–18)

This is hare-hunting. But in *Twelfth Night* there is a reference to foxhunting with hounds when Sir Toby says, 'he is now at a cold scent', and Fabian answers: 'Sowter will cry upon't for all this, though it be as rank as a fox' (II, v, 124). And Master Ford speaks of bolting a fox from its earth in terms familiar to the modern ear, in *The Merry Wives of Windsor*:

> I'll warrant we'll unkennel the fox. Let me stop this way first. So, now uncape.
> (III, iii, 151)

Uncape means put the terrier down the earth.

Slender and Page in this play are both coursing men, and Page has a very good greyhound, which he runs at the Cotswold hares (*Merry Wives of Windsor* I, i, 81–8). This also is one of the delights offered to the deluded Sly in *The Taming of the Shrew*:

> Say thou wilt course, thy greyhounds are as swift
> As breathed stags, ay, fleeter than the roe.   (Induc. ii, 48–9)

Here is a reminder that deer as well as hares were coursed, but this could only be managed after considerable preparation, in a park divided into 'courses' as at Windsor. It was perhaps just possible to follow a coursing match after hare on foot, but after buck one had to be mounted.

Park hunting itself was inseparable from poaching, and Shallow, who has a park and delights in sending his friends presents of venison, accuses Sir John Falstaff of beating his keepers, killing his deer and breaking open his lodge, though not of kissing his keeper's daughter (*Merry Wives of Windsor* I, i, 103–5). But the interesting thing is that his own kinsman Slender who is so proud of the family's gentle rank is reputed in his own youth to have fought with a warrener, that is, to have had an affray with someone else's keeper, no doubt when trespassing in pursuit of game. The game-preserving class was also the poaching class, or part of it.

Yet another reference to coursing is made by Berowne in *Love's Labour's Lost* (IV, iii, 1) who also mentions 'toils' or nets used in park hunting. In an earlier scene the Forester (head-keeper) shows the Princess the 'stand' from which she may make the fairest shoot (IV, i, 10). In *The Comedy of Errors* (II, i, 100–1) there is a more complicated reference to park hunting involving the use of a stalking horse ('stale') by the keeper. It is true that 'stale' could also mean prostitute but it is wrong to gloss it so in this passage where Adriana implies that her erring husband can only be approached under cover of her. The implication is that her husband, a 'stag', has broken out of the park and is devouring some farmer's crop. Therefore the keeper must shoot him. (It is a lot of fuss about nothing; all the poor man has done in fact is to go out to lunch with some business friends.) Again, in *As You Like It* (V, iv, 105), the Duke says: 'He uses his folly like a stalking-horse, and under the presentation of that he shoots his wit.' The keepers are actually seen at work that might well have involved the use of a 'stale' in *III Henry VI*, where Act III opens in 'A chase in the north of England', as it might be Bishopdale Chase.

Enter two Keepers, with cross-bows in their hands.

First Keeper: Under this thick-grown brake we'll shroud ourselves,
                    For through this laund anon the deer will come;
                    And in this covert will we make our stand,
                    Culling the principal of all the deer.
Second Keeper: I'll stay above the hill, so both may shoot.
First Keeper: That cannot be, the noise of thy cross-bow
                    Will scare the herd, and so my shoot is lost.   (III, i, 1–7)

Although the crossbow was silent enough for poachers to use, since it could not be heard as far off as the parker's lodge, its twang was loud enough to unsettle the deer.

FALCONRY: THE LANGUAGE OF VENERY

The hunting of smaller ground game did not necessarily involve riding, but coursing did and so did most branches of falconry. Few people, in Shakespeare's England, owned a firearm accurate enough for use as a 'birding piece' with which one could shoot flying game, and neither the crossbow nor the longbow were suitable for this purpose. Thus the niche among field sports now occupied by shooting was then filled by falconry, though for the pot great reliance was placed on netting and liming and the use of decoys and snares, not only by professional wildfowlers.

Both hunting and falconry had an immense technical vocabulary which can be found expounded in such works as George Turberville's *Noble Art of Venerie or Hunting* (1575). This dialect was Norman-French in origin and was more or less internationally current, at a certain social level, throughout Western Europe. The majority of horses bred by and for the rural gentry were intended to be ridden, at

Falconry by pillion from the *Playfair Book of Hours* illustrating May, Hawking. (Victoria and Albert Museum; reproduced by permission of the Conway Library, Courtauld Institute of Art)

some time, out hunting or hawking. For this, the requirement was not so much speed or the ability to jump as endurance, handiness and a comfortable ride. They must not be too tall because more mounting and dismounting was involved then than now. Pictures of Elizabethan hunting men show them mounted on what are virtually ponies.

Talking of hawking; nothing else, my lord.   (*II Henry VI* II, i, 52)

It is just as well there is something else, or the interpreters nowadays would have a hard time of it. For of all the several dialects of the language of venery, hawk-talk is the least widely comprehended today. There are not many people in St Albans now, let alone members of the Abbey Theatre Club, that can make head or tail of all this dialogue about flying at the brook (duck-hawking), or could comprehend all those points and pitches and towerings. We do gather, however, that a high wind was not considered the ideal hawking weather. Again, Sly is offered the choice of falconry for his day's recreation as a lord:

Dost thou love hawking? Thou hast hawks will soar
Above the morning lark . . .

(*The Taming of the Shrew*, Induc. ii, 44–5)

Falconry had always been, at least in Western Europe, a social activity very favourable to courtship. You will see far more miniatures of mixed parties out

Falconry German style. This was a completely international art. Woodcut from Fugger, *Von der Gestüterey*, 1584. (Reproduced by permission of Miland Publishers, Nieuwkoop, Netherlands)

hawking, in illuminated manuscripts, than of mixed hunting parties. I can think of at least one in which the demoiseau has a hawk on his first and a peach of a demoiselle on the pillion behind him. The kind of idyll that begins like this is found with Florizel and Perdita in *The Winter's Tale*:

> I bless the time
> When my good falcon made her flight across
> Thy father's ground.   (IV, iv, 14–16)

But behind the jolly hours spent at the brookside or in the open fields or 'at the bush' there lay, on someone's part, many weary hours of nerve-racking training, spent in 'manning' the hawks, as young eyasses 'coy and wild as haggards of the rock' (*Much Ado* III, i, 35–6), by sitting up all night and staring them in the eye; sometimes also by weakening them with hunger, as Petruchio had done in his time:

My falcon now is sharp and passing empty,
And till she stoop she must not be full-gorg'd,
For then she never looks upon her lure.
Another way I have to man my haggard,
To make her come and know her keeper's call;
That is, to watch her, as we watch these kites
That bate and beat and will not be obedient.

(*The Taming of the Shrew* IV, i, 177–83)

Of course nobody ever 'manned' kites, carrion birds useless for falconry. 'Kite' was simply a term of abuse levelled impatiently at a falcon, meaning any useless raptorial bird.

Again, one does not put too much reliance on the textual criticism of the computer. But the fact that there are more than forty separate references to falconry in the total of the works must be some measure of the part which this sport played in the lives of the kind of people on whom the characters in the plays were modelled. I would include among these the disputed passage in *Hamlet* (II, ii, 375) about when the wind is south. Hamlet is much more likely to need to distinguish hawk from hernshaw (the normal falconer's term for a heron) than from a handsaw. 'Cry havoc', which occurs more than once in Shakespeare, is also a term from falconry. It was about the one native English word in the predominantly French vocabulary of the falconer: 'Hafoc', the Anglo-Saxon word for hawk, uttered at the moment when the falcon was thrown up after the game.

14

War

Which should sustain the bound and high curvet
Of Mars's fiery steed.   (*All's Well* II, iii, 278–9)

The speaker is Parolles, 'the gallant militarist ... that had the whole theoric of war in the knot of his scarf' (IV, iii, 137). He is quite useless as a soldier, is a coward and a liar, and when taken prisoner (as he thinks) is ready to divulge the whole strength and organisation of the Florentine army at the first threat his captors utter. But his whole success as a courtier – and he gets away with it for a long time, right down to Act IV, Scene iii – is his ability to speak the military language accurately, consistently, fluently, credibly. Verbally he is invincible – does not his very name mean 'words'? So that when he associates the warhorse with the very 'airs above the ground' (*courbette*) which are still practised in the Spanish Riding School of Vienna and by the Cadre Noir of Saumur, we may be certain that real soldiers also believed these acrobatics to be an essential accomplishment of the charger. Surely they, even that military mountebank Parolles, must have known more about it than the theorists of our day who maintain that the bounds and high curvets never had any practical purpose in warfare.

So one would think: but very powerful vested interests worked to impose such exercises on the military establishment. The sphere in which they were accounted of use – not to weary the reader with an explanation of just how they could be employed to the discomfiture of the enemy – was in the actions of first-line cavalry such as is referred to as simply 'horse' in the order of battle of the Florentine army which Parolles recites blindfold to his interrogators.

This was still the prestige arm of the service, everywhere. Its command, even when it formed numerically a small part of the army, was an index of eminence in

Robert Devereux, Earl of Essex and Earl Marshal of England, on his charger. (Reproduced by
courtesy of the Board of Trustees of the Victoria and Albert Museum)

the military hierarchy. When Bertram, Count of Roussillon, therefore, is named
General of the Florentine horse, that means he is the Lieutenant-General, next in
seniority to the Captain-General or Commander in Chief. In real life, cavalry of
this kind was coming to play a less and less decisive role; indeed it had been
something of an anachronism for nearly a century, in England at least. Horse, as
Shakespeare understood it, was still essentially what it had been in the Wars of the

Kerne meant light-armed soldiery, not necessarily mounted. Here we see one acting as groom to an Irish chief, the horse wearing the characteristic stirrupless Irish saddle. The groom carries the eight-foot-long 'horseman's staff' instead of a lance. John Derricke, *The Image of Ireland*, 1581, Pl. I. (By permission of the Syndics of Cambridge University Library)

Irish cavalry withdrawing in the face of English troopers who have curb bits, whereas the Irish have snaffles and no stirrups. In the background dismounted kerne wearing 'strait strossers' likewise withdraw before English musketeers and halberdiers. John Derricke, *The Image of Ireland*, 1581, Pl. IX. (By permission of the Syndics of Cambridge University Library)

Roses, or for that matter in the wars of Henry IV and V: the practical manifestation of chivalry, the personal service rendered by peers and their dependants in arms, side by side with the gentlemen of the royal household. This was the reason why command of 'the horse' was an appointment of such prestige – not so much that it gave the opportunity of doing more damage to the enemy as because its ranks were filled, in theory, with illustrious personages. Even though, ever since the middle fourteenth century, those ranks had been increasingly filled, in reality, by skilled and unprincipled mercenaries, the fiction was still politely maintained. The wonder is that the institution had lasted so long, for the lance with which these knight-substitutes were armed was not effective except in the hands of the Spaniards, whose technique in this respect was quite different from that of the English or the French. As for the armour which covered the lancer cap-à-pie, it was not shot-proof, nor quarrel-proof, and even the old-fashioned clothyard arrow could still search out its weaknesses. That tired old pro, the knight in his military capacity, was still speaking his lines with less and less conviction in the European theatre of war when *All's Well* was first produced – probably about 1604 – and his ghost still walked on in the English Civil War forty years later, there to be laughed off the stage at his farewell performance.

There were two other kinds of mounted troops in English and Continental armies which did much more of the real work of the battlefield but whose existence would barely be guessed at on the evidence supplied by Shakespeare in his works. There was light horse, which performed more the functions which we think of today as the true role of cavalry as we last saw it – reconnaissance and harassing roles. English light horse tended not to be English. Troops of this kind would be represented at their best in quality, and most abundantly in quantity, in the combined forces of that peripheral coalition in *Henry IV*: Douglas, Percy, Glendower. They were to be found in Wales – the Welsh Cob was developed specially for their use – and in all that part of Scotland between the Lammermuirs and Galloway. They were also to be found, of necessity, in the English counties bordering those regions, such as Herefordshire – whence Mortimer led 'the power of the county' against Glendower – Northumberland, Durham and Cumbria. Traditionally this Northumbrian light horse had never been committed in Continental wars because it was on permanent stand-by in case of hostilities against the Scots, and this factor remained a real one until 1603. For similar reasons light horse from the Marches Against Wales was never deployed in the old battleground of France and the Low Countries so long as a Welsh incursion remained a likely contingency – almost until the lifetime of the Queen's grandfather. But they did serve in the Irish wars, together with Welsh light horse and archers. Conversely, for a campaign in France or the Low Countries it had been the policy to engage

German mercenaries, 'shot on horseback'. Woodcut from Fugger, *Von der Gestüterey*, 1584.
(Reproduced by permission of Miland Publishers, Nieuwkoop, Netherlands)

Irish light horse, which had two advantages: as mercenaries, their rate of pay was
very reasonable; and it suited the English Crown to keep Irish fighting men out of
Ireland in one way or another. Large numbers of them were in fact in the service of
Henry V at the siege of Harfleur, though all we hear of them from Shakespeare is
that rather blue remark of the Dauphin's: 'you rode, like a kern of Ireland, your
French hose off, and in your strait strossers'* (*Henry V* III, vii, 53). The Irish
officer Macmorris appears in *Henry V*, somewhat untypically, as a sapper miner.

* Narrow trousers, the only mention in Shakespeare of such garments, would be much more practical for the
  purpose than the Dauphin's alternative, French hose, which could only be worn on horseback with thigh-high
  Cordovan boots to avoid chafing.

At the real-life siege of Harfleur he would be much more likely to command a troop of light horse or 'kerns'.

The second kind of mounted troops were what Shakespeare's contemporaries called 'shot-on-horseback'. By his time there were probably no more mounted archers anywhere in Britain: mounted arbalesters still existed, though it had never been the custom in the English army to shoot with any kind of bow from the saddle. A keen and cranky militarist called Sir John Smith wrote a closely argued pamphlet, in Shakespeare's lifetime, urging the authorities to go back to late classical antiquity and train squadrons of shot-on-horseback to shoot arrows from the saddle at the gallop as the Huns and the Parthians had done, and as the Turks and Tartars still did. This art once mastered, Sir John contended, would give England the edge over all potential enemies, but above all it would save the exchequer the horrible expense of powder and shot. As things were, only pistoleers fired from the saddle; calivermen dismounted to shoot. Between them, these were the ancestors of the dragoons who in the following centuries came near to supplanting true cavalry in the English army. They were the successors, in function, of those German *Reuters* whose employment in England had been one of the more unpopular acts of the Queen's father: 'Joly Rutterkin' had been a cordially hated figure in John Skelton's England. The quality of horses assigned to this arm of the service, as later to dragoons, was notoriously the worst. Anything sound on three legs and having the sight of one eye would do to carry a brace of pistols.

Of Irish light horse it is Edmund Spenser, not Shakespeare, who has most to say at this time. But what he says of their horses at length, William Camden said more succinctly: 'Their horses likewise (we call them hobies) are very excellent; they go not as other horses do but amble very soft and easie.' The light-horseman, of whatever origin, was also called a 'hobilar' because he rode a hobby, which we have already met in Chapter 1. There was in fact only one kind of horse to be had in Ireland at this time – what we now call a Connemara pony and what was then called a hobby. It was used by all classes of the population for all purposes, varying in quality and hence in price, but all of one stamp. More particularly, none of them trotted, and this was one of the features that distinguished light horse from cavalry of the line: the chargers of the latter *must* trot as is made clear from all ordinances of this time regarding the requisitioning of remounts. But light-horse remounts need not do so; easy-ambling hobbies would do for them. They would also do to mount captains of foot companies, who customarily rode on the march, though lieutenants and ensigns went afoot. The infantry officer's horse was a vehicle and not a charger.

Just as in peace the horse was a mobile throne, so in war it constituted a mobile command-post. Whether or not he chose to engage personally in the hurly-burly of

Great Seal of James I. (The British Library)

close combat, the Captain-General was mounted, by an unquestioned tradition, on a horse of the same stamp as that ridden by the cavalry of the main battle, but of course a little better. That still meant, in terms of Elizabethan warfare, on the most superior grade of armour-carrying charger – either an Andalusian or a Neapolitan. The logical and most absurd extreme of this concept is the representation on his Great Seal of James I, that most pacific of monarchs, in full armour with closed helm, broad sword and all, mounted on a great ramping war-stallion.

All the world knew that he was a dedicated horseman, but only because his favourite recreation and almost only form of exercise was hunting, which demanded a different sort of horse altogether.

◊ ◊ ◊

The horses that loom so large in the military episodes of Shakespeare's plays are of course all chargers rather than troop horses. The dramatist thought of warfare, whatever the historical setting of his plot, as it was practised in his own day by the English army. Thus, broadly speaking, officers of every period and nationality were to him either 'captains' or 'great captains', because in the Elizabethan army every senior commander was first and foremost the Captain of a company that was in a sense his property, though in battle it might never come under his eye from dawn to dusk of a long day's action fought under command of his Lieutenant. After all, what is a Lieutenant for but to *tenir lieu* for the Captain? The rank which we call 'General' was the '*Captain*-General', and still is in the Spanish army, which as a professional force was acknowledged to be of surpassing excellence by all Englishmen of military experience in Shakespeare's day. In England today, we still have a Captain-General of Marines.

The eminence from which the great captain of real life dominated the battlefield was seldom a topographical feature like the windmill of Crécy, but rather the saddle of a tall horse. Of this fact every dramatist who put a battle on the stage was only too painfully aware. There was no way of getting a horse on to the stage, access to which was by stairs or ladders. Yet battles there had to be, as they were such good box-office. Besides, if the management own a cannon, they want it to be shooting off a peal of ordnance about once a month, even if the play is about dark-age Denmark (*Hamlet*), or the siege of Angers (*King John*) at the wrong end of the thirteenth century for fireworks.

So let the cannon earn its keep: go bid the soldiers shoot, and fairly often. The modern film impresario presenting any of the histories and most of the tragedies has no hesitation in introducing a strong element of the horse opera because he is freed from the besetting limitation that hampered all London managers around 1600. Once he has put his Antony or his Richard III on horseback he is faced with a comparatively simple choice. He can, for the sequences in which the horse is in motion, turn the rider's back to the camera and substitute a stunt man or woman. Or he can photograph the star full-face, sometimes giving an atrocious display of horsemanship which only a minority of the audience are in a position to criticise.

Because this was not possible at the Globe, compensation was sought and found in the rich descriptions of the chargers of various warlords, persons of the dramas.

Laurence Olivier as Richard III on White Surrey at the head of his army. White Surrey is here acted by a horse which looks in front like an Andalusian and behind like an Arab. It is quite probable that in the year of Bosworth (1485) this type of horse would be readily available from Spanish sources. What would not be available anywhere is the horse on the left – so manifestly a half-bred hunter – because there was no Thoroughbred to breed such animals from. (Crawford Films)

I can think of only one working dramaturge who had the wit to exploit this drawback by making some very telling lines of copy from it – not so much an apology as a defiance:

> Think, when we talk of horses, that you see them
> Printing their proud hoofs i' the receiving earth.
>
> (*Henry V* Prologue, 26–7)

This was one of the ways in which the 'gentles all' were invited to suspend their disbelief and imagine that the cockpit could 'hold the vasty fields of France' (Prologue, 11–12), their fancies to behold 'Upon the hempen tackle ship-boys climbing' (III, Chor., 8). In fact it was just possible to present this, shipboys and all, on the stage if the action demanded it. But when a horse appeared in the theatre, as the celebrated black Barb stallion Marocco did when performing his act under the management of Mr Bankes, the fore-stage had to be dismantled and the theatre stripped down to the state in which it was used in its alternative capacity as Bear Pit.

But apart from such mechanical difficulties it would not have been feasible, as was done occasionally in the nineteenth and early twentieth centuries, to present on horseback on the stage certain characters in situations where, as everybody knew, they would in real life have been mounted. The overriding consideration

Mount suitable for a crowned head. Woodcut from Fugger, *Von der Gestüterey*, 1584.
(Reproduced by permission of Miland Publishers, Nieuwkoop, Netherlands)

was that no theatrical company had among its assets one single horse of anything near the quality that would be ridden by Henry V or Richard III or Othello, or Tamburlaine for that matter, at moments when his life depended on the performance of his horse. One can only think of one instance where a genuine (ex-)royal horse of this calibre appeared in the theatre, and that was long after Shakespeare: after George III died his superb Hanoverian cream 'Adonis' was sold to Astleys to appear in the equestrian drama *Mazeppa*, but being then upwards of twenty years old and correspondingly cheap even he must have stretched the audience's credibility a little. The Globe audience might accept a treble-voiced choir-boy as the King of France's daughter because in default of actresses this was part of the game. But they would never have accepted the manager's town hack ('street nag') in the role of White Surrey; they knew too much. Whereas your modern television audience will swallow a four-mouth-old foal as born last night, without straining.

But the author of *Henry V* knew how boring unrelieved talk about horses could be. Has he not given us, in the Dauphin, the champion horse-talking bore of all time? Although we are spared the sonnet the Dauphin wrote to his incomparable animal, we are spared little else; none of the clichés. In the middle of his eulogy (*Henry V* III, vii, 11–45), there is a fair sample of the 'intellectual' concepts about the natural history of the horse that bedevilled veterinary theory, and horse-breeding through it, as much in the reign of Elizabeth I as of Henry V. 'He is pure air and fire' – that is, two of the four possible elements that could prevail in the 'temperature' of a horse, and the two most desirable. These elements, as was proper, also dictated the colour of the coat, which in this case was between bay and chestnut – 'the colour of the nutmeg' – found frequently in the Andalusian, as we see from both Velázquez and Van Dyck. To be clear of the less desirable and most unwarlike elements of earth and water which 'never appear in him, but only in patient stillness while his rider mounts him . . .', all one had to do was to avoid horses with white (but not grey) and unmarked black coats respectively. (One wonders what on earth Richard III was doing ordering White Surrey to be saddled for the field on the morning of Bosworth (V, iii, 65), unless the author really meant to imply that his protagonist was already losing his grip, bringing out his parade horse to ride into the thick of the mêlée.)

The technical equipment of dramatic critics in the post-mechanical age can be measured by the way most of them evaluate in terms of poetic imagination the Dauphin's talk on the night before Agincourt concerning his horse. In fact it contains every contemporary bromide in the book, skilfully assembled and arranged. Even the lines starting 'Your mistress bears well' (*Henry V* III, vii, 46) are derived from an English résumé of qualities desirable in a horse, current in Shakespeare's day, full of *double entendre* and applicable also to women; it ends: 'and easy to leap upon'.

Of the troop-horses of the rank-and-file in the 'main battle', who were mounted and armed still as armoured lancers – 'men-at-arms' – in the late medieval manner, we hear nothing in the plays, nor of their counterparts in the militia, that one in ten of all 'hable men' in a parish who must turn out when summoned 'with hors and harneys' to make up 'the powers of the counties'.

In *I Henry IV* (II, iv, 339–42), we have a fair description of the kind of horsemanship practised on both sides of the Borders Against Scotland, when Falstaff and the Prince are talking about Douglas 'that runs a'horseback up a hill perpendicular – He that rides at high speed, and with his pistol kills a sparrow flying.' This was the kind of military horsemanship that foreigners never saw in

'Behold the ordinance on their carriages.' (Reproduced by courtesy of the Trustees of the British Museum)

action, because all such feats were performed in the bitter intermittent guerilla struggles that smouldered between the Tees and the Forth for centuries between the Roman occupation and 1603. This was the reason why the Northumbrians had the name of 'the finest light horse in England' until the end of the seventeenth century, but in fact by then they had long ceased to deserve it. In practice their decline was swift, final and irrevocable by the time Shakespeare had ceased to write for the stage. By an ordinance of the third year of his reign, King James I destroyed the formidable Border light horse, as well English as Scots, by disarming all the inhabitants of the frontier zone and forbidding any of them to own a horse worth more than £2 – and as we saw in Chapter 11 above the only other minority against which the government discriminated in the same terms was the luckless recusants.

Of English light horse in the Continental wars we hear something in *I Henry VI*, where Talbot says:

> He fables not; I hear the enemy.
> Out, some light horsemen, and peruse their wings.   (IV, ii, 42–3)

A little vague? Well, after all, he *is* the Captain-General. It is up to some diligent staff-officer to specify *which* light horse, and how many. But this is just what in our day – or yesterday – was considered the true function of light horse: reconnaissance or fighting for information.

Horse artillery, in the true sense of batteries drawn by horses, with all the gunners mounted so as to march at the speed of cavalry, did not exist in the day of Shakespeare, but field artillery, horse-drawn, with gunners afoot, was known. By one of his customary anachronisms he makes the chorus in *Henry V* invite us to 'Behold the ordinance on their carriages' (III, Chor., 26) which implies horse-drawn pieces, though in fact at the time of Agincourt there was no 'carriage' off which the gun could fire. Henry V's field pieces were the same as his castle pieces, transported in ox-carts and lifted on to static wooden mountings before firing. This is the only instance in Shakespeare where 'carriage' is a concrete noun meaning essentially an axle and two wheels. But Henry V was in his grave before the gun-carriage was invented and gunners got fewer ruptures.

The same Chorus in the following Act mentions among the night sounds of the camp that 'Steed threatens steed, in high and boastful neighs' (IV, Chor., 10), which made silence before attack, and hence surprise, practically impossible. The medieval squire's nightmare was civil war breaking out in the lines where the first-line chargers were picketed, and this passage reminds us that, one and all, they were still literally the Anglo-Saxon 'stedas' or stallions. In theory, if no mare were present they would do no more than threaten, but it only needed a shift of the wind to bring the scent of a horsing pack-mare from the baggage-lines. Such a fracas in the picket-lines had begun a chain of events which ended in the defeat of the Christian forces by the Turks at Nicopolis in 1396 (as my friend and colleague Miklos Jankovich has reminded me), and regrettable incidents of this nature were a commonplace for another hundred years after Nicopolis. Finally in the reign of Henry VII English armies adopted the practice of the Hungarians in using geldings, if not as chargers, at any rate for the rank and file of light horse and shot-on-horseback. But there was still an absolute veto on mares in their ranks, or in those of the rapidly dwindling heavy armoured 'horse', justified thus by Enobarbus:

> If we should serve with horse and mares together,
> The horse were merely lost.   (*Antony and Cleopatra* III, vii, 7–8)

Shot-on-horseback from the Northern border counties, who were an ungentlemanly, businesslike sort of mounted infantry, rode geldings almost exclusively, as did their Lowland Scots counterparts. Indeed the best of their horses were the fast and enduring Galloways, usually referred to as 'Scotch trotting geldings'. The word 'Galloways' only occurs once in Shakespeare, spoken by Falstaff's henchman Pistol. 'Know we not Galloway nags?' he says, about someone who is small but of high nuisance value (*II Henry IV* II, iv, 186). As long as the Border reivings lasted, the men of Galloway were the most feared by the English, partly because they lived not just across the Border but off to one side, behind the Solway Firth, and were thus less open to reprisals. They therefore did not hesitate to commit atrocities of a kind which raiders living in, say, Berwickshire, would avoid for fear that some day they might be called to account. That is how the London theatre audience thought of the Galloway horse whose riders were quick in manoeuvre and most tireless in long cross-country marches by day and by night, throughout the reign of Elizabeth I. Yet from early in the century following the Union of Crowns, and progressing quickly thereafter, English breeders of 'running horses' plucked from this Galloway nettle, danger, a flower that was not exactly safety but something almost as precious to them. For besides being the only indigenous breed fast enough to race itself, the Galloway provided, among the foundation mares of what was to become Thoroughbred bloodstock, an unknown number of anonymous dams that seem to have added a unique catalytic to the mixture of Oriental strains. Many other countries crossed Arabs, Turks, and Barbary horses with their fastest home-bred mares, but apparently because they had no Galloways, none of them achieved a result comparable with *le pur-sang anglais*.

The officer's charger throughout the works is most often called a courser, a usage on which we have commented above. As a poetic convention it was becoming more and more widespread. Yet one sees no instance of it in prose works, whether technical or not, whether civil or military. The standard requirement for remounts, other than for light horse or shot-on-horseback, was always expressed as a 'great trotting horse', but this phrase never occurs in Shakespeare.

I do not subscribe to the view that Shakespeare had ever been a soldier; only that he had rubbed shoulders with many men who had served in the wars by land and sea. Nor do I hold that his view of warfare is an idealised drum-and-trumpet one. Act IV of *Henry V* shows the contrast: on the one hand there is militaristic bombast, the (usually civilian) jingoist glorification of the morning of battle, when

> The sun doth gild our armour; up, my lords! . . .
> Hark, how our steeds for present service neigh!   (IV, ii, 1, 8)

On the other hand is the reality, put into the mouth of that hard-boiled veteran Grandpré. As the champions stagger out of their corners for the last round, groggy and punch-drunk, he sees the sick and exhausted English knights on their deadbeat horses, sitting

> . . . like fixed candlesticks,
> With torch-staves in their hand; and their poor jades
> Lob down their heads, dropping the hides and hips,
> The gum down-roping from their pale-dead eyes,
> And in their pale dull mouths the gimmal'd bit
> Lies foul with chaw'd grass, still and motionless;
> And their executors, the knavish crows,
> Fly o'er them all, impatient for their hour.   (IV, ii, 45–52)

This is the way days of battle really dawn, at the end of a campaign in any country or age, for men and for horses.

15

Racing

Although horse-racing of a sort had existed in England since the Middle Ages, even those who would endow it with the most respectable lineage do not pretend that it amounted to much before the reign of James I. It was not, in general, the sport of kings – hunting was. There were monarchs now and again who displayed some interest in it, such as Richard II, but Queen Elizabeth I took a good deal less notice of it than Queen Elizabeth II does. And she spent comparatively little money on what Edward Topsell, in his *Historie of Foure-Footed Beastes* (1607), called 'Coursers or swift light running horses'. Probably the majority of races before 1600 remained what they had been originally, a prelude to horse fairs, part of the 'show' in which the quality of the goods about to be sold (or at least offered) was displayed. The expression 'jockey', not used by Shakespeare himself, seems to have become current in his lifetime and to have been applied to a rather low class of 'horse-courser', usually Scots or North Country, who hung about fairs and got casual employment with dealers, either running-up in hand or riding the horses he had for sale. You can see what Ben Jonson understood by a jockey in *Bartholomew Fair*.

What races there were often had a field of only two runners, being essentially 'matches' between two owners arranged entirely for their satisfaction. 'I have *heard* of riding wagers', says Imogen (*Cymbeline* III, ii, 72). She was a member of the court circle (and let it be repeated here that the court of Cunobelinus is thought of as no different from the court of King James), yet she had never *seen* a race.

You can scrape the barrel till you come to the splinters but you will not find more than a handful of references to this pastime throughout Shakespeare's works.

There is Imogen's speech just quoted from *Cymbeline*. A brief allusion in *Hamlet* 'not to crack the wind of the poor phrase, running it thus' (I, iii, 108–9) is more likely to belong to racing than to any other activity, even though broken wind can be acquired by other means than racing and training. 'Running' at this period meant galloping, though earlier it had meant something else.

The word 'swoopstake', an earlier form of sweepstake, occurs once, in *Hamlet* (IV, v, 142), and there is a baffling passage in *The Winter's Tale*:

> You may ride's
> With one soft kiss a thousand furlongs ere
> With spur we heat an acre.   (I, ii, 94–6)

There are only two clues. Races are measured in furlongs. The word 'heat' in this scene was employed in early racing, when the entire field did not run at once, but in heats eliminating for the final, as in modern athletics. We can find no analogue for 'heat an acre', but as an acre is theoretically (hardly ever in practice) a strip in the common field a furlong in length by four rods or poles or perches in width, a heat in a race or trial for it might have consisted in galloping round an acre, the circuit of which would have measured a minimum of two furlongs eight rods. Quarter-mile horse-races existed in America in colonial times (and still do today) – were they perhaps based on the old-country tradition of heating (round) an acre? One way or another, we are assisting here at the birth of racing lingo.

The very scantiness of this evidence leads to the conclusion that racing bored the dramatist, or else that the majority (or even the most influential minority) in his audience had no interest in the sport. The nearest thing to it that gets the full treatment is coursing, which once meant racing, but did so no more in Shakespeare's day, and is dealt with in Chapter 13 above.

16

Daily life in the stable

The principles governing the housing of horses were well understood, and have been described by several authors of the time, so that although probably not a single stable of Shakespeare's day is still in existence as such in the whole country, and although this was the least frequently painted architectural subject, we yet have a fair idea of what the Elizabethan stable was like. The most obvious difference between then and now was the complete absence of the loose-box – an invention of eighteenth-century Newmarket. All horses stood in stalls or in sheds.

A synthesis of contemporary written sources gives the following specifications for ideal stabling. The site should be on dry and rising ground, the approaches not to be muddy; close to running water, yet remote from ponds or other stagnant water. It should not be haunted by other livestock such as poultry or pigs, and indeed should stand apart from pigsties and henhouses, and likewise from privies. It should not be open to the roof, but ceiled over, so that dust was less likely to lodge in rack and manger. The hayrack should be high and the manger strong and deep enough to prevent horses wasting corn by tossing it out. The floor should be level, not sloping up towards the manger, and of paving stones or cobbles, not planking. Plenty of windows, all provided with movable shutters, should be provided. The saddle room, in more pretentious households, should lie between the stable itself and the lodging of the grooms, and should contain besides saddles and bridles a kit of tools for running repairs as well as veterinary instruments and 'medicinable things'. Security was more of a factor, in relation to the feedhouse, than it is now; more stress was laid on locking the oat-bin against thieves from without or pilfering from within the household by servants than on a design that would keep the corn from mouldering. There must be separate buildings for storing hay, straw and used litter (the practice among grooms of sweeping soiled litter into a sort of glory-hole under the very large mangers must have been widespread, as it is so frequently condemned by writers). A covered sand-bath was necessary for horses to roll in after work, which of course they would not be able to do in a stall. Sheds, often without sides, were to be provided where horses could be groomed without the resultant dust, hairs and scurf getting into their feed and drink. Nicholas Morgan is almost alone in recommending isolation quarters for sick horses, though he only stipulates a shed, which we should now consider unsuitable for hospital purposes.

How close, and how often, reality came to the ideal, we can only guess. But in all probability this layout was only found at the country residences of the nobility, and not at all of them. Hygienic housing standards for horses are not likely to have been widespread among a class which itself was only a few generations removed from the regime in which the floor of the great hall was covered, under the latest application of rushes, by a sort of deep litter rich in apple-cores, gnawed bones, and the excreta of hawks and hounds among others. The stable yards of town houses, even those of the rich, would not permit the amount of elbow room described, and the ground plans of London palaces of the period do not show enough space to accommodate so many separate buildings. Urban ground came very expensive by the square foot. Ventilation especially is likely to have fallen very far short of the desired standard. As late as the nineteenth century, hand-books on stabling draw attention to the fondness of conservative horsekeepers for dark and closely air-stopped stables. Mud-free approaches, again, were a counsel of perfection: it went without saying, in the world of William Shakespeare, that horse and man returned from every journey covered either with dust or mud according to the weather.

Work and tools

The removal of manure, the increasingly burdensome bugbear of the modern horsekeeper, is likely to have been less troublesome to urban horsekeepers in the age of Shakespeare, since all arable farmers and market gardeners suffered from a chronic shortage of muck, with no chemicals and little inorganic dressing being used on the land. Thus plenty of contractors would be willing to empty the lay-stall free of charge in most towns; but not, it seems, in Cambridge, where the under-graduate Lord Cranborne kept a horse in 1607 and had to pay the scavenger an outrageous sum for removing horse-dung. But perhaps this was part of the well-known university policy of discouraging persons *in statu pupillari* from keeping horses (now cars) in term.

The equipment of the stable in the reign of the first Elizabeth differed very little

Not the ideal stable. Rubens, *The Prodigal Son*, 1618. (Koninklijk Museum voor Schone Kunsten, Antwerp)

from that used in the days of the second, barring the fact that some of the old tools are now made of different materials. Thus both dungforks and pitchforks for handling hay and straw had wooden tines, not iron as now. This had the advantage of greatly reducing the accident risk, and must have cut down the incidence of tetanus materially. Buckets were mostly leathern, sometimes wooden. It was not customary to leave water in the stall, but to lead the horses to water several times daily.

The technique of grooming was the same then as now. It was invented a long time ago, and the detail of Assyrian bas-reliefs show the troopers of King Assurbanipal going through all the motions performed by grooms of the sixteenth century and of today. Only the various kinds of brush in use today were much less often seen, since in pre-mechanical days a brush, as opposed to a broom or besom, was a rather expensive hand-made object. The only brushes commonly used on horses were made of hedgehog-skin, and were so rough and sharp that their use was strictly limited. More reliance was placed on the wisp and the human hand. There were no hoses, so it was more important to have access to a deep pool of clear water with a hard bottom, if there were no pump or well. The bath (*Pferdeschwemme*) like an outsize sheep-dip, big enough to swim a horse in, which was common in Central Europe at that time, seems to have been unknown in England. Even Hampton Court did not have one.

Feeding

Fodder and forage were sold in measures now unfamiliar to us, so that it is hard to visualise, from accounts, what the customer was getting for his money. Standards were still not uniform throughout the country. Both the gallon and the stone could contain a different number of pints or pounds according to whether they were measured at Hull or at Halifax. There were two weights called quarters: 25 lb (not 28 as now), because it was a fraction of a 'short' hundredweight, and 5 cwt (long), being a quarter of a ton. Hay and straw were sold by the bottel, which was a bundle rather than what we should call a bale but, to judge by the amount of feeds it was made to provide, a bottel of old hay seems to have weighed about 28 lb. In bulk it was almost always accounted for by the load, which is utterly baffling until one realises that there was a theoretical standard load of seventy-two bottels. If of old hay this would weigh 18 cwt; and this implies, not a wagonload, but the capacity of a two-wheeled cart extended by lades which were unshipped when carrying less bulky loads. In the first decade of the seventeenth century hay was being bought and sold in Hertfordshire, the county which supplied most hay to London, at 34s the load, which is about 37s 9d a ton. This means that hay was a relatively expensive commodity. But in good years it could be obtained for as little as 29s a ton.

Oats cost about 2s 6d a 'long' hundredweight, but this was not so important then as now, since it was not the major form of protein given to horses. Peas and beans, dried and crushed, were fed either loose with chaff or made up into horse-loaves by the 'brownbaker'. These loaves might also contain rye, barley or other meal.

In the England of today, 'the stables' in daily parlance are usually either a riding school or a livery yard, frequently of the 'do-it-yourself' variety. 'Hiring' establishments as such are few and far between. As we saw in Chapter 4, in Shakespeare's England hiring stables were almost always in inn-yards, whether or not the inn was a post house. Postmasters let out horses for a standard day's journey in standard directions. To hire a horse for any other purpose than travelling the official 'stage' you would have to apply elsewhere, looking for a house, almost certainly an inn, with a sign inscribed 'in such great letters as they write "Here is good horse to hire"' (*Much Ado* I, i, 246). The Garter at Windsor was such a house, and the landlord not being a postmaster could make his own terms for hire and was not bound to a statutory scale of charges (*Merry Wives of Windsor*). Postmasters did not need these 'great letters' as they already displayed the sign of the horn. Together with the use of a 'fat and bean-fed horse' – bean-fed, anyway – you would obtain the services of a groom of the stable. Bridegrooms apart, groom only meant 'servant', the *simple soldat* of domestic service; in great houses there were grooms of practically everything (even of the close-stool), and in the grandest houses the stable department had at its head a Master of the Horse, then a Gentleman of the Horse (sometimes more than one), assisted by some Gentlemen Riders and by the principal non-commissioned officers such as the Yeoman of the Horse and the Yeoman of the Coche, and it was under their eye that the Grooms of the Stable worked. 'I was a poor groom of thy stable', says the lad who used to do Roan Barbary, coming to visit Richard II in prison (V, v, 72). The grooms in *Macbeth* never touched a horse: they were of the bedchamber.

Normally horses were taken to the forge to be shod, and only very large establishments had their own smithy. Even the innumerable offices grouped round the stable yard of Syon House in 1633 did not include a smithy. But there was never a township without its smith, and though the accomplishment is very desirable nowadays, it was really superfluous in Portia's suitor, the Neapolitan Prince, who:

> makes it a great appropriation to his own good parts that he can shoe him himself. (*Merchant of Venice* I, ii, 40)

He was a crashing bore of almost Dauphin standard who fortunately never comes on stage. If he did, he would no doubt treat the audience to a disquisition on the farrier's art as practised by himself, 'a colt indeed' (I, ii, 39).

The greatest number of 'sumter' or packhorses kept at this time by tradesmen belonged either to millers, to brewers or to maltmasters, and 'malt-horse' was a recognised type of very strong, not very fast animal with great weight-carrying potential. A burly but stupid man was always prone to be called a 'whoreson malt-horse drudge', as in *The Taming of the Shrew* (IV, i, 114) Petruchio calls Grumio.

That some of the stables had planked floors we may deduce from *King John*, where the Bastard Faulconbridge says: 'To crouch in litter of your stable planks' (*King John* V, ii, 140).

In the absence of brushes the groom of the stable might be thankful if his charges did not carry a full tail. Docked horses were quite common and seem to have occurred rather haphazardly up and down the social scale. Docking then had no particular connection with harness work as it had until latterly, before being forbidden by English law. One is almost ashamed to trot out Bay Curtal again from his comfortable stable in *All's Well*; but, poor jade, he is very useful in so many different roles. So then for the third time: Curtal was the commonest name for docked horses, and this one belonged to Lord Lafeu who obviously thought highly of him and rode him in expensive 'furniture' (*All's Well* II, iii, 59). Docking (curtailing) was something of an economic sacrifice when you consider the industrial implications: so many more objects were made of horsehair in that century than in ours — all sorts of cords and ropes from the finest fishing-lines up to boat rigging. A great many harness parts including wainropes and countless domestic objects such as bed-cords were spun out of it. The manes and tails of dead horses did not suffice, and it was customary in many parts of the country, as it is in Spain to this day, to crop the mane and tail hairs of horses at that season when they grow fastest, in order to use or sell the hair. If you amputated the dock you deprived yourself of about half this useful by-product. Ergo, in general, poor men did not dock.

The special horse-loaves made by the brownbaker are mentioned, rather obliquely, in *Measure for Measure*. Lucio confides to the supposed Friar (really the Duke) that the Duke would, despite his affected prudery:

> mouth with a beggar though she smelt brown bread and garlic. (*Measure for Measure* III, ii, 177)

No doubt beggars did very often eat horsebread, but so did the poor in general, well above the level of mendicancy, for the difference between it and the coarsest kind of bread for human consumption was a legal rather than a physical one.

Cardinal Wolsey on one of his two mules of state. (Bodleian Library, Oxford, MS. Douce 363, fol. 52v)

Another possible occupant of the stable, tucked into a corner out of the way, was a donkey, then invariably called an ass. Donkeys were fairly common in Shakespeare's London, but almost unknown in some parts of the country. Despite *Measure for Measure*'s 'ass whose back with ingots bow' (III, i, 26) we can find no evidence at this period of donkeys working for Cornish tinners or North Pennine lead-smelters, who used pack-ponies extensively. It is possible they may have worked in the Sussex iron-fields. Wherever used, donkeys were housed less frequently than horses; from the start, the English had failed to appreciate that the ass originating in semi-desert Barbary would not live in the open exposed to rain and cold, or breed, without progressive loss of stature from one generation to another. The English ass of that day was a dwarf compared to the Spanish ass of the same origin. The words of the thirteenth-century friar, Bartholomew the Englishman, had been taken too literally by his countrymen; he wrote in *De Proprietatibus Rerum*: 'he may away with travail and thralldom, and useth vile meat and little, and gathereth his meat among briars and thorns and thistles'. A bottel of hay at something like 5d was by no means vile meat, but the last thing the English donkey was likely to taste. No wonder the transmuted Bottom longed for one: 'good hay, sweet hay, hath no fellow' (*A Midsummer Night's Dream* IV, i, 33).

Alternatively, lodging in some uncomfortable corner, there might be a mule that earned his living by doing the dirty work of the establishment. It would no doubt be small, chance-bred, the fruit of some regretted *mésalliance*. And not at all handsome, for by this time in England mule-breeding had become a lost art, the demand having been cut off sharply at the Reformation. Anyone over eighty at the first performance of *King Henry VIII* might remember having seen Cardinal Wolsey in progress mounted on a magnificent mule. In Catholic Western Europe then and for long after, the accepted mount for bishops, abbots and above was a mule, but of such quality as is rarely seen today. The breeding formula was out of an Andalusian mare by a Catalan jackass. There was a good sale for them to senior ecclesiastics. The great Chancellor had two such, each in the care of a 'mewleter', as George Cavendish tells us in his *Life of Cardinal Wolsey*, adding an illustration that shows one of them. This among other points has been taken to imply that Shakespeare had read Cavendish before writing *Henry VIII*, though in fact the *Life* had not yet been printed but circulated widely in manuscript, notably among Catholic families. There we find:

> and grew so ill
> He could not sit his mule.   (*Henry VIII* IV, ii, 15–16)

All stables had their share of deceitful horses, like Brutus' 'hollow men', who:

> . . .like horses hot at hand
> Make gallant show and promise of their mettle;
> But when they should endure the bloody spur
> They fall their crests and like deceitful jades
> Sink in the trial.   (*Julius Caesar* IV, ii, 26)

This can be seen at any modern hunter-trial. These are the opposite of 'honest' horses, now more often called 'genuine'. 'Fall their crests' brings us back in full circle to Chapter 1 above, and Shakespeare's employment of the now secret, but then open, horse lexicon within the English language. Only the initiated now know what is meant by an honest horse; and few suspect that 'crest-fallen' was once also a technical term for a disability of horses, specifically of stallions, for which there were reputed veterinary cures.

L'Envoy

And now, gentles all, if you have read thus far 'you shall know all, that you are like to know' (*Midsummer Night's Dream* V, i, 117), or at least all that I can discover, about this actor who never actually trod the boards of the Globe, the Mermaid, the Rose, the Hope or the Swan; but yet was always waiting in the wings. I believe there is a green-room tradition that it is unlucky to quote from *Macbeth*; nevertheless I cannot think of a more appropriate way of taking leave of you than with the words of that sanguinary thane:

> I wish your horses swift, and sure of foot;
> And so I do commend you to their backs.
> Farewell.   (III, i, 37–9)

St Pierre-de-Chignac
Dordogne

Danby Dale
North Yorkshire

Groom using curry comb. Woodcut from Fugger, *Von der Gestüterey*, 1584. (Reproduced by permission of Miland Publishers, Nieuwkoop, Netherlands)

Bibliography

This bibliography lists mainly those works which are referred to or quoted from in the text, thus taking the place of a note or reference system within the text itself.

Bartholomaeus Anglicus [Bartholomew the Englishman]. *De Proprietatibus Rerum*. English translation by John Trevisa. Cologne, 1472.

Batho, G. R. (ed.). *The Household Papers of Henry Percy, Ninth Earl of Northumberland (1564–1632)*. Royal Historical Society, Camden. London, 1962.

Berners, Dame Juliana. *The Boke of St Albans*. St Albans, 1486. 'The properties of a good horse.'

Blundeville, Thomas. *The Fower Cheifest Offyces of Horsemanship*. London, 1565.

Browne, W. *Browne His Fiftie Yeares Practice*. London, 1624.

Camden, William. *Remains concerning Britaine*. London, 1605.

Cavendish, George. *Thomas Wolsey, Late Cardinal; His Life and Death*. London, 1588. Reprinted Folio Society, London, 1962.

Cavendish, William (Duke of Newcastle). *A General System of Horsemanship*. Antwerp, 1658. Facsimile of 1743 edn printed 1970.

Crofts, J. *Packhorse, Waggon and Post*. London, 1967.

Dekker, Thomas. *The Gull's Hornbook*. London, 1609. Facsimile edn Scolar Press, Menston, 1969.

Dent, Anthony. *Chaucer and the Horse*. Proceedings of the Leeds Philosophical and Literary Society, vol. IX, part I, December 1959.

Dent, Anthony. *Cleveland Bay Horses*. London, 1977.

Duhousset, Lt. Col. E. *The Gaits, Exterior and Proportions of the Horse*. London, 1896.

Fugger, Marcus. *Von der Gestüterey*. Augsburg, 1584.

Grisone, Federigo. *Ordini di Cavalcare*. Vinegia, 1553.

Jankovich, Miklos. *They Rode into Europe*. Trans. A. Dent. London, 1971.

Jenkins, J. Geraint. *The English Farm Wagon: Origins and Structure*. Newton Abbot, 1961 (3rd edn 1981).

Manwood, John. *A Treatise of the Lawes of the Forest*. London, 1615. Facsimile edn Amsterdam/New Jersey, 1976.

Markham, Gervase. *A Discource of Horsemanshippe*. London, 1593.

Melling, Elizabeth (ed.). *Kentish Sources: a Collection of Examples from Original Sources in the Kent Archives Office*. Maidstone, 1959–.

Morden, Robert. *The New Description and State of England*. 2nd edn, London, 1704.
Morgan, Nicholas. *Perfection of Horsemanship*. London, 1609.
Moryson, Fynes. *An Itinerary*. London, 1617. Facsimile edn Amsterdam, 1971.
Prior, C. M. *The Royal Studs of the Sixteenth and Seventeenth Centuries*. London, 1935.
Rastell, John. *The Statutes*. London, 1527.
Rhys, Ernest. *Latimer's Sermons*. Everyman's Library. London, [1906].
Ruellius, Johannes. *Veterinariae Medicinae libri duo*. Basel, 1537.
Saxton, Christopher. *An Atlas of England and Wales*. London, 1579.
Sedgwick, Adam. *A Memorial, by the Trustees of Cowgill Chapel with Preface and Appendix on the Climate, History and Dialect of Dent*. Cambridge, 1868.
Skelton, John. *The Complete Poems*. London, 1931.
Spenser, Edmund. *A View of the State of Ireland*. Dublin, 1633.
Stokes, William. *The Vaulting Master, or the Art of Vaulting Reduced to a Method*. London, 1641 and Oxford, 1652.
Stow, John. *A Survey of London*. London, 1598. Reprinted Oxford, 1971.
Topsell, Edward. *Historie of Foure-Footed Beastes*. London, 1607.
Turberville, George. *The Noble Art of Venerie or Hunting*. London, 1575.
Turton, R. B. *The Honour and Forest of Pickering*. North Riding Record Society, 1896.

ARCHIVES

Cecil Papers, Hatfield House.
College of Arms, MS.M.6. 'A Book of Ceremony showing the Order of March for the Accession Procession of Queen Elizabeth I'.
North Yorkshire wills, Northallerton, Record Office.

668/05